Florida

State Assessments
Grade 5
Science

SUCCESS STRATEGIES

**FSA Test Review for the
Florida Standards Assessments**

D1261715

BOCA RATON PUBLIC LIBRARY
BOCA RATON. FLORIDA

Dear Future Exam Success Story:

Congratulations on your purchase of our study guide. Our goal in writing our study guide was to cover the content on the test, as well as provide insight into typical test taking mistakes and how to overcome them.

Standardized tests are a key component of being successful, which only increases the importance of doing well in the high-pressure high-stakes environment of test day. How well you do on this test will have a significant impact on your future, and we have the research and practical advice to help you execute on test day.

The product you're reading now is designed to exploit weaknesses in the test itself, and help you avoid the most common errors test takers frequently make.

How to use this study guide

We don't want to waste your time. Our study guide is fast-paced and fluff-free. We suggest going through it a number of times, as repetition is an important part of learning new information and concepts.

First, read through the study guide completely to get a feel for the content and organization. Read the general success strategies first, and then proceed to the content sections. Each tip has been carefully selected for its effectiveness.

Second, read through the study guide again, and take notes in the margins and highlight those sections where you may have a particular weakness.

Finally, bring the manual with you on test day and study it before the exam begins.

Your success is our success

We would be delighted to hear about your success. Send us an email and tell us your story. Thanks for your business and we wish you continued success.

Sincerely,

Mometrix Test Preparation Team

Need more help? Check out our flashcards at: http://mometrixflashcards.com/FSA

Copyright © 2016 by Mometrix Media LLC. All rights reserved.
Written and edited by the Mometrix Exam Secrets Test Prep Team
Printed in the United States of America

TABLE OF CONTENTS

Top 20 Test Taking Tips

1. Carefully follow all the test registration procedures
2. Know the test directions, duration, topics, question types, how many questions
3. Setup a flexible study schedule at least 3-4 weeks before test day
4. Study during the time of day you are most alert, relaxed, and stress free
5. Maximize your learning style; visual learner use visual study aids, auditory learner use auditory study aids
6. Focus on your weakest knowledge base
7. Find a study partner to review with and help clarify questions
8. Practice, practice, practice
9. Get a good night's sleep; don't try to cram the night before the test
10. Eat a well balanced meal
11. Know the exact physical location of the testing site; drive the route to the site prior to test day
12. Bring a set of ear plugs; the testing center could be noisy
13. Wear comfortable, loose fitting, layered clothing to the testing center; prepare for it to be either cold or hot during the test
14. Bring at least 2 current forms of ID to the testing center
15. Arrive to the test early; be prepared to wait and be patient
16. Eliminate the obviously wrong answer choices, then guess the first remaining choice
17. Pace yourself; don't rush, but keep working and move on if you get stuck
18. Maintain a positive attitude even if the test is going poorly
19. Keep your first answer unless you are positive it is wrong
20. Check your work, don't make a careless mistake

Copyright © Mometrix Media. You have been licensed one copy of this document for personal use only. Any other reproduction or redistribution is strictly prohibited. All rights reserved.

Physical Sciences

States of matter

The three states of matter are **solids**, **liquids**, and **gases**. In a solid the **atoms** or **molecules** of a substance are close together and locked into place. The solid has a definite shape and volume. In a liquid the atoms or molecules are farther apart. A liquid flows and takes the shape of its container. In a gas the atoms or molecules are very far apart and have a lot of energy. They will fly completely way if not held inside a container like a balloon or a closed bottle.

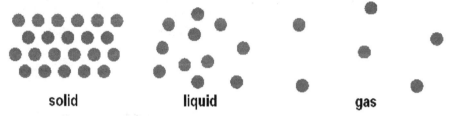

solid   liquid   gas

Intensive and extensive physical properties of matter

Intensive properties are those that do not depend upon the size of the sample. Examples are density, melting-freezing point, boiling point, color, chemical reactivity, luster, malleability, and electrical conductivity. Extensive properties do depend on the size of the sample. Examples include the amount of space occupied (volume), mass, and weight. Note that mass and weight are not the same thing. Mass is the amount of material present in a body, whereas weight is the gravitational force acting upon that mass in a specific gravitational field. A 100-kilogram object has the same mass on Earth as on the Moon, but its weight will change markedly. It will weigh 980.7 Newtons (220.5 pounds) here on Earth, but only 163.5 N (36.75 lbs) on the Moon. In outer space this object would weigh nothing at all, but would still have a mass of 100 kg.

Transfer of heat between systems or objects

Heat transfer occurs through radiation, conduction, and/or convection. Radiation transfers heat energy by electromagnetic waves, and is how solar energy is transported across the vacuum of space from the Sun to Earth. The other two forms of heat transfer involve particle motion in physical media. Conduction transfers heat energy through collisions between adjacent particles. As molecules gain heat they acquire more kinetic energy and move faster. When they collide with neighboring particles, some of this kinetic energy is transferred, which causes the neighboring particles to begin to move faster. Some substances such as metals are much better conductors of heat than others, such as down, which has numerous empty air spaces. Convection occurs when the flow of a warm fluid carries heated material from one place to another. This is seen in boiling water and the convection currents in the atmosphere or Earth's mantle.

Copyright © Mometrix Media. You have been licensed one copy of this document for personal use only. Any other reproduction or redistribution is strictly prohibited. All rights reserved.

Water

States of matter for water

The solid state of water is **ice**. Ice cubes float around in a glass of water and do not change their shapes except by melting. When ice melts it becomes **liquid water**, which can flow and take the shape of its container. This is true of all liquids. When liquid water evaporates into **water vapor** or boils away as **steam** it becomes a gas. A gas completely fills its container.

Ice floats in liquid water

Density is the mass (amount of matter) in a certain volume. The more matter there is, the more the object weighs. Most solids have more matter than the same volume of their liquids. This means that they are denser and sink in their own liquid. However, water is different. The molecules in ice are farther apart than they are in liquid water. That means that ice has less matter in it than the same volume of liquid water. Therefore, ice is less dense and floats in water.

Magnet

A magnet is a metal or object that produces a magnetic field. A magnetic field is mapped by invisible curved lines of force that attract magnets or certain metals like iron or nickel. A simple bar magnet has a south pole (S) at one end and a north pole (N) at the other. Each pole will attract the opposite pole of another magnet and repel the same pole. The north pole of a compass needle will point to the south pole of a magnet, while the south pole of the needle will be attracted to the north pole of the magnet.

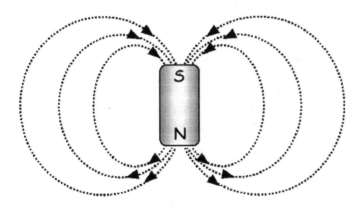

Copyright © Mometrix Media. You have been licensed one copy of this document for personal use only. Any other reproduction or redistribution is strictly prohibited. All rights reserved.

Opposite poles of two magnets attract each other

When two bar magnets are lined end to end with the north and south poles near each other, the lines of force run from the north pole of one magnet to the south pole of the other magnet indicating attraction.

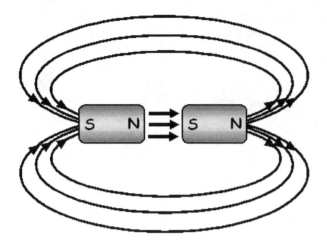

Cutting a bar magnet in two

If a bar magnet is cut in two, two complete magnets will form, each with a north and south pole. If a bar magnet is cut it into three parts, three magnets will form.

Poles of two magnets repel each other

When the like poles of two magnets are brought close to each other the lines of force run in opposite directions. This causes the two poles to push each other away.

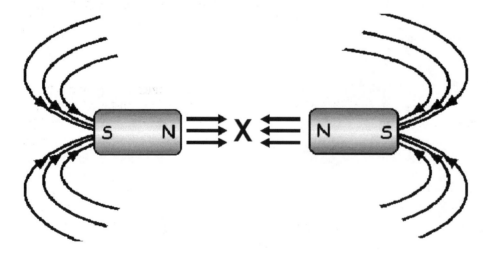

Copyright © Mometrix Media. You have been licensed one copy of this document for personal use only. Any other reproduction or redistribution is strictly prohibited. All rights reserved.

Needle of a magnetic compass

Planet Earth has a magnetic field just like a bar magnet. The north pole of a compass needle points to Earth's north pole because the magnetic pole near the North Pole is actually the south pole of Earth's magnetic field. Likewise, the south pole of the compass needle is attracted to the north pole of Earth's magnetic field near the south geographic pole. Just remember that each magnetic pole is attracted to its opposite pole on another magnet or magnetic object.

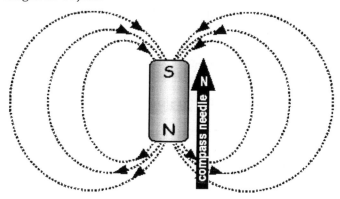

Physical changes

Physical changes are those that do not affect the chemical properties of a substance. Changes in state are physical changes. For example, a liquid can freeze into a solid or boil into a gas, but its chemical nature remains the same. Ice, steam, and liquid water are all still water (H_2O). Physical properties include features such as shape, texture, size, color, odor, volume, mass, and density, although some changes in color or odor can indicate chemical changes. Certain changes such as the dissolution of ionic or polar compounds in a solvent are considered physical changes even though they involve breaking chemical bonds. If a saltwater solution evaporates, crystalline table salt will be left behind as a precipitate; adding water will produce a new saltwater solution.

Chemical changes

Chemical changes occur when chemical bonds are broken and new ones are formed. The original substances are transformed into different substances. If vinegar and baking soda are mixed together, a lot of bubbles (carbon dioxide) and water will form. Burning wood in a fireplace is another type of chemical change. The carbon in the wood reacts with oxygen in the air to make ash, carbon dioxide, smoke and energy that we feel as heat and see as light.

A chemical change occurs when two or more substances come together and interact in such a way that they become different substances. For example, two hydrogen atoms and one oxygen atom combine to make a new compound—a water molecule, H_2O. Likewise, two oxygen atoms and one carbon atom combine to make one molecule of carbon dioxide—CO_2. The two substances that combine are called **reactants,** and the new compound that emerges is the **product. Chemical reactions** (changes) can be much more complicated than this.

Copyright © Mometrix Media. You have been licensed one copy of this document for personal use only. Any other reproduction or redistribution is strictly prohibited. All rights reserved.

Examples of chemical changes include the following: (a) The temperature of a system changes without any heating or cooling. (b) The formation of a gas (bubbles). (c) The formation of a precipitate (solid) when two liquids are mixed. (d) A liquid changes color.

Chemical changes occur when chemical bonds are broken and new ones are formed. The original substances are transformed into new compounds or elements, and energy is released or absorbed. For example, methane can combine with oxygen to produce carbon dioxide, water, and energy: $CH_4 + 2O_2 \rightarrow CO_2 + 2H_2O$ + energy. Similarly, an acid (sulfuric acid) and a base (sodium hydroxide) can combine chemically to form a salt (sodium sulfate) plus water: $2 NaOH + H_2SO_4 \rightarrow 2H_2O + Na_2SO_4$. The rusting of iron (oxidation) is a chemical change, as is the decomposition of water into oxygen and hydrogen when an electric current passes through the water: $2H_2O$ + electricity $\rightarrow 2H_2 + O_2$. In each case, the original compounds or elements (reactants) are transformed into new compounds (products) that were not originally present.

Classical states of matter

The three classical states of matter are solids, liquids, and gases. Solids have a definite volume and density at a given temperature and pressure, a degree of structural rigidity and a constant shape, and a resistance to flow. However, some solids such as modeling clay can flow and undergo deformation under pressure. Liquids also have a definite volume and density at a given temperature and pressure, but they flow readily and do assume the shape of their container. However, a liquid will only occupy the portion of a container that is equal to its volume. A gas is far more diffuse than even a liquid, and will expand to fill the entire volume of its container. The molecules are spread much farther apart, and they move more rapidly and randomly than in a liquid.

Chemical compound

A chemical compound consists of two or more different elements with a fixed ratio of atoms. These atoms are held in a specific arrangement by covalent, ionic, or metallic bonds. Substances formed from two or more atoms of a single element are not considered compounds. Examples are diatomic hydrogen, oxygen, nitrogen, and chlorine (H_2, O_2, N_2, Cl_2) or polyatomic molecules such as O_3 (ozone), P_4, and S_8. An example of a compound is when two hydrogen atoms and one oxygen atom combine to form water (H_2O). Other examples of compounds include: two hydrogen atoms, one sulfur atom, and four oxygen atoms combine to form sulfuric acid (H_2SO_4); two oxygen atoms and a carbon atom come together to make carbon dioxide (CO_2); and four hydrogen atoms and a carbon atom combine to form methane (CH_4).

Balancing a chemical reaction

In a chemical equation, it is necessary to have the same number of atoms for each element on each side of the equation. Reactants appear on the left side of the equation and the products appear on the right. The elements are balanced by placing the necessary coefficients in front of each element or compound. In a simple example, diatomic hydrogen (H_2) combines with diatomic oxygen (O_2) to form water:

$H_2 + O_2 \rightarrow H_2O$

Copyright © Mometrix Media. You have been licensed one copy of this document for personal use only. Any other reproduction or redistribution is strictly prohibited. All rights reserved.

Adding up all the atoms for each element shows that there is one more oxygen atom on the reactant side than the product side of the equation. Since water contains twice as many hydrogen atoms as oxygen atoms, placing the coefficient 2 in front of both the hydrogen molecule on the reactant side and the water molecule on the product side balances the equation:

$$2\,H_2 + O_2 \rightarrow 2\,H_2O$$

Again, count the number of atoms of each element on both sides of the equation. There are 4 hydrogen atoms and 2 oxygen atoms on each side of the equation so it is balanced.

Motion

Motion can be (a) **straight line motion** like the train shown here, (b) **circular motion** like Earth revolving around the Sun, or (c) **back and forth motion**, like the weight **oscillating** at the end of a spring.

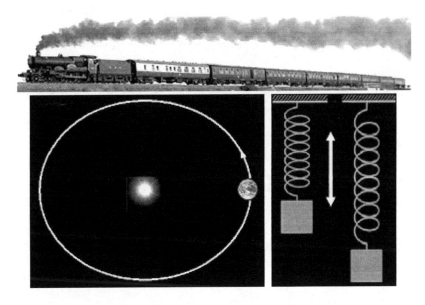

Newton's Third Law of Motion

Newton's Third Law states that every **action** has an equal and opposite **reaction**. Whenever you push on an object (exert an action) such as a wall, for example, the wall pushes back directly against you with exactly the same force (the reaction). That equal and opposite force exerted by the wall against your hands and arms is the resistance you feel. As long as your action and the wall's reaction are balanced, no net force is exerted and neither you nor the wall move: $\vec{F}_1 = -\vec{F}_2$. However, if the "wall" is a flimsy bamboo curtain, you can easily push it aside or knock it over. The bamboo curtain's inertia is not adequate to counteract the force you applied. A net unbalanced force acts against it, which causes it to accelerate (move). Now, Newton's Second Law applies. This law is expressed with the formula $\vec{F}_{net} = ma$, which states that force equals mass times acceleration.

Copyright © Mometrix Media. You have been licensed one copy of this document for personal use only. Any other reproduction or redistribution is strictly prohibited. All rights reserved.

Newton's Second Law of Motion

Newton's Second Law states that the force operating on a body is equal to the body's mass times its acceleration: $F = ma$. It applies to situations in which there is a net unbalanced force. If the net applied force is sufficient to overcome the body's inertial and frictional forces of resistance, the body will accelerate (change its direction and/or speed of motion). The degree of acceleration will be directly proportional to the applied force and inversely proportional to the body's mass. This is shown graphically below.

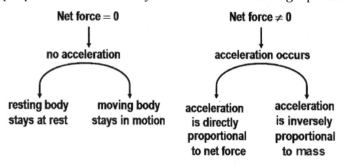

Levers

A **lever** is a simple machine made up of a rigid rod or beam that rotates on a fixed pivot or **fulcrum**. It can be used to lift a heavy mass by applying a small force over a large distance at one end to exert a much larger force over a shorter distance at the other end. Seesaws, crowbars, and shovels are all levers. Increasing the length of the lever arm decreases the necessary force required to lift the weight. A lever is a simple machine.

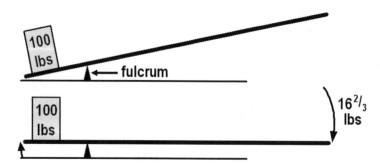

Inclined planes

An **inclined plane** is a flat surface with one end raised higher than the other— like a ramp. It works similar to a lever. By pushing a heavy object over a longer distance (the inclined plane), the object can be raised a shorter distance in height with a smaller force than it would take to lift it straight up. The longer the inclined plane, the less force is required to raise the object. This is also a simple machine.

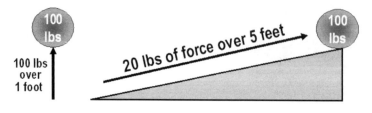

- 8 -

Copyright © Mometrix Media. You have been licensed one copy of this document for personal use only. Any other reproduction or redistribution is strictly prohibited. All rights reserved.

Screws

A screw is another kind of simple machine. It turns rotational force (the turning of the screw) into forward or linear force that makes the screw bore into wood or other substance. The screw is an inclined plane wrapped around a central nail. The force of turning the screw with a screwdriver acts along the longer distance of the spiral inclined plane to penetrate a shorter distance into the wood. It takes less force to turn the screw than to hammer a nail into the wood.

Wedges

Still another kind of simple machine is a wedge, like an axe or a knife. A wedge concentrates and converts a downward force into a sideways force. It cuts down into an object and pushes the sections to the side. A nail is also a wedge.

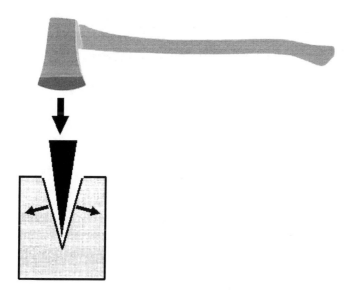

Copyright © Mometrix Media. You have been licensed one copy of this document for personal use only. Any other reproduction or redistribution is strictly prohibited. All rights reserved.

Wheels and axles

A wheel and axle is a type of simple machine. A wheel is basically a large circular lever attached to a much smaller axle. By applying a small force to turn the wheel a longer distance around the wheel, a much larger force is given to the smaller diameter axle. A doorknob is an example. The wider the knob the easier it is to open the door latch.

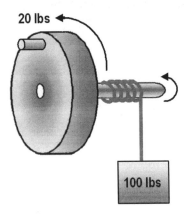

Pulleys

A pulley is one or more wheels with grooved rims through which a rope or cable runs to change the direction of pull and lift a load. With just a single fixed pulley the amount of force needed to lift a weight is the same as the weight. But if a second moveable pulley is added as shown here, the amount of force needed to lift the weight is cut in half — just 50 pounds.

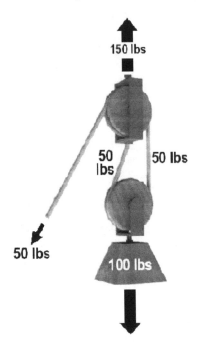

Liquid water vs. ice

There is a difference in state. The water in the glass is a liquid, while that in the pail is a solid. The liquid water flows and takes the shape of its container. The solid ice does not flow

- 10 -

Copyright © Mometrix Media. You have been licensed one copy of this document for personal use only. Any other reproduction or redistribution is strictly prohibited. All rights reserved.

and does not assume the shape of the pail. The ice is also less dense than the water and will float in the water.

Complex machines

A complex machine is a machine that combines two or more simple machines. For example a pair of scissors is made up of two wedges acting in opposite directions connected by a lever.

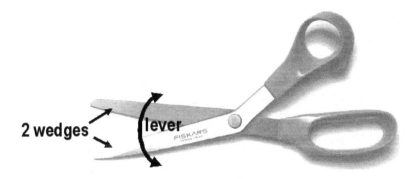

Wheelbarrows

A wheelbarrow is a complex machine. It is a lever mounted on a wheel and axle.

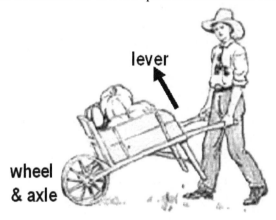

Saw

A saw is actually a complex machine. Each tooth in a saw blade is a wedge. Therefore, a saw consists of many wedges, which makes it a complex machine. When a person saws a piece of wood, he exerts both a downward force and a back and forth force. This cuts into the wood and pushes the two sides apart just like an axe.

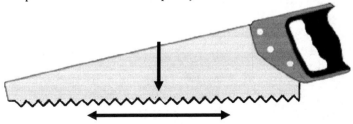

Copyright © Mometrix Media. You have been licensed one copy of this document for personal use only. Any other reproduction or redistribution is strictly prohibited. All rights reserved.

Hot air balloons

When the air inside a balloon is heated it expands and makes the balloon swell up. The air inside the balloon is now lighter than the same volume of air outside the balloon. That is because the same volume of air outside has more matter (air) than the air inside the balloon. This heavier air sinks down around the balloon as shown by the arrows and pushes the balloon up (vertical arrow). Because helium is also lighter than air, a helium balloon floats, too.

$E = mc^2$

This is Einstein's famous equation showing the equivalence between energy and matter. E is the amount of energy in a system, m is its mass equivalent, and c is a constant: the speed of light in a vacuum (3×10^8 m/s, or 300 million meters per second). This is the basis for the atomic bomb. A huge amount of energy can be released by converting a very small amount of matter multiplied by the speed of light squared: 9×10^{16} m²/s². As an example, one kilogram of matter can be converted into 9×10^{16} kg m²/s², which is equal to 90,000 trillion joules. This is the explosive equivalent of 21.5 megatons of TNT.

Temperature scales

The three main temperature scales are Fahrenheit, Celsius, and Absolute, or Kelvin. The first is used mainly in the United States, while the Celsius scale is used in the rest of the world and in science. The Absolute scale is used almost exclusively by scientists. The following formulas can be used to convert temperatures from Fahrenheit to Celsius, and from Celsius to Fahrenheit:

$°C = \frac{5}{9}(°F - 32)$; $°F = \frac{9}{5}(°C) + 32$

The Absolute scale is based on the Celsius scale. One kelvin (one K) is equal to one degree Celsius. The difference is that zero is set at absolute zero (= −273.15 °C) instead of at the freezing point of water. Absolute zero is the temperature at which all atomic and molecular motion stops and matter as we understand it would cease to exist. This temperature can never be reached in the real world, although scientists have come within a few billionths of a degree of reaching it in the laboratory. Even in outer space, the microwave background radiation has a temperature of 2.725 K (−270.425 °C).

Converting absolute zero into degrees Fahrenheit
0 K = −273.15 °C; $°F = \frac{9}{5}(°C) + 32 = \frac{9}{5}(−273.15 °C) + 32 = −459.67°F$

Copyright © Mometrix Media. You have been licensed one copy of this document for personal use only. Any other reproduction or redistribution is strictly prohibited. All rights reserved.

<u>Mercury thermometer</u>
Elemental mercury is an ideal thermometer material. At a given pressure, it evenly and reversibly expands when heated and contracts when cooled. A fixed amount of mercury is sealed inside an evacuated tube and a calibrated temperature scale is attached. This scale is calibrated by fixing the boiling (100 °C or 212 °F) and freezing (0 °C or 32°F) points of water at 1 standard atmosphere of pressure (760 mm Hg). The distance between these two points is divided using 100 or 180 evenly spaced lines, depending on whether the temperature will be measured in Celsius or Fahrenheit. These divisions are continued above and below these points to expand the scale above boiling and below freezing. As the mercury heats up it expands at a constant linear rate and its volume increases uniformly. The mercury column rises and falls in the tube according to the temperature, which can be read directly from the attached scale.

Electrical circuit

An electrical circuit is a closed path within which electrons can flow from a power source (a battery or alternator) through a conducting medium such as an insulated copper wire (or salt water) to a load (such as an incandescent light or other electrical appliance) and back to the power source or "ground." When the connections are complete, the current flows. When they are broken (such as when a switch is turned off), the current ceases to flow. Electrical current can do work against the circuit's resistance to the current flow, including the resistance of the copper wire and the mechanical and other resistance in the appliance (e.g. the amount of heat necessary to make a metal filament in an appliance glow and emit light).

Structure of an atom

A neutral atom consists of an extremely dense nucleus composed of one or more positively charged protons and (except for hydrogen-1) a varying number of uncharged neutrons. The nucleus is surrounded by a cloud of one or more negatively charged electrons that are equal in number to the protons in the nucleus. The protons and neutrons are bound together by the strong nuclear force, which is stronger than the repulsive force between the positively charged protons. The negatively charged electrons are attracted to the positively charged protons by the electromagnetic force. The number of protons determines the identity of the chemical element, while the number of electrons in the outermost shell determines the ways in which the atom interacts chemically with other atoms or molecules.

Molecule

A molecule is an electrically neutral combination of two or more atoms joined by covalent bonds. Molecules can be as simple as diatomic hydrogen or oxygen (H_2 and O_2) gas or water (H_2O), or as complex as large biochemical macromolecules such as proteins, starches, and cellulose. Ions (electrically charged atoms that have unequal numbers of protons and electrons) are joined by ionic bonds, and are not considered molecules. An example of an ion is simple table salt. Metals are not considered molecules either. They consist of positively charged ions that are in a sea of unattached and unlocalized electrons.

Copyright © Mometrix Media. You have been licensed one copy of this document for personal use only. Any other reproduction or redistribution is strictly prohibited. All rights reserved.

Light year

A light year (ly) is the distance light will travel in a vacuum in one year. It is a common measure of astronomical distances. Since light travels in empty space at 300 million meters per second, the distance it will travel in one year is equal to $\frac{3\times10^8 m}{1\,s} \times \frac{1\,km}{10^3 m} \times \frac{60\,s}{1\,min} \times \frac{60\,min}{1\,hr} \times \frac{24\,hr}{1\,day} \times \frac{365\,day}{1\,yr} = 9.46 \times 10^{12}\,\frac{km}{yr}$. This is close to 9.5 trillion kilometers in a year (about 5.9 trillion miles per year). It should be noted that a light year is a unit of distance, not time. Another astronomical measure of distance is the parsec, which equals about 3.26 light years, or approximately 31 trillion kilometers.

Materials denser than water

Ships and other floating objects made of materials that are denser than water float because of the empty space they contain inside their hulls. A ship weighing 5,000 tons overall will displace 5,000 tons of water, but this weight of water will occupy a smaller volume than the ship itself. Once this amount of water has been displaced the ship will not sink any deeper into the water and will float. Archimedes' principle states that the buoyant force is equal to the weight of the water (or any other fluid displaced). The reason a solid piece of iron or a rock sinks is that it weighs more than the volume of water it displaces. For the same reason, because a helium-filled balloon is lighter than air it will rise until the air's density is reduced such that the volume of air displaced is the same as the volume of the balloon.

Prism

White light is what we see when all of the colors in the visible spectrum are present in the right proportions. It is the color of the light produced by our Sun, incandescent and fluorescent lamps, and white-emitting light-emitting diodes (LEDs). When white light passes through a prism it is separated into its component colors. For humans, the visible color spectrum ranges from violet through blue, green, yellow, orange, and red. Humans see electromagnetic wavelengths from about 390–570 nanometers, corresponding to frequencies of 400–790 trillion cycles per second (terahertz). Longer wavelengths and lower frequencies have lower energies than shorter wavelengths and higher frequencies. They also scatter less and travel farther in transparent media (such as air or water). Light from the setting Sun has farther to travel through air than when it is higher in the sky. Red light penetrates better than the other colors and so sunsets appear red.

Alternate energy resources

There are several different alternative energy choices including wind, solar, hydroelectric, geothermal, and biofuels. Wind energy is harnessed by the use of large wind turbines. These turbines convert the kinetic energy from the wind into electrical power. Solar energy is energy derived from the radiation emitted by the sun. A variety of techniques and technologies are used to capture this energy, but the processes typically involve large banks of solar collection panels. Hydroelectric energy is generated by the flow of water. It is usually captured using water turbines placed in an area where there is a naturally occurring high volume of water flow, such as a large waterfall, or where a manmade structure such as a dam creates a store of potential energy. Geothermal energy is heat energy generated by the earth's core. It is usually harnessed by heating water to create steam, which is then used to turn turbines that generate electricity. Biofuels are fuels that consist of organic material

Copyright © Mometrix Media. You have been licensed one copy of this document for personal use only. Any other reproduction or redistribution is strictly prohibited. All rights reserved.

from previously living creatures. The mass of these previously living creatures is known as biomass, and it is the primary component of biofuels.

Copyright © Mometrix Media. You have been licensed one copy of this document for personal use only. Any other reproduction or redistribution is strictly prohibited. All rights reserved.

Life Sciences

Typical plants

A typical plant has three major sections; roots, stems, and leaves. The **roots** lie underground where they absorb water and minerals needed by the plant. These water and minerals are carried up to the leaves through special tubes in the **stem** or **trunk**. The **leaves** use the water from the roots and absorb carbon dioxide from the air. The green color in **leaves** is due to **chlorophyll**. Chlorophyll absorbs sunlight to produce a special chemical that releases energy to enable the plant to produce sugar to nourish the rest of the plant. This food-making process is called **photosynthesis**.

Flowers

Flowers are the structures which many plants reproduce. A typical flower has both male and female parts. The male **stamens** consist of a stalk called a **filament** with a swollen **anther** at the tip which produces the **pollen**. The female parts consist of an **ovary** which produces the seeds and a tube called a **pistil** through which the pollen enters to fertilize the seeds. Showy colorful **petals** surround the male and female parts. Below the petals are smaller **sepals** that are usually green.

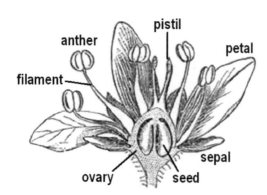

Copyright © Mometrix Media. You have been licensed one copy of this document for personal use only. Any other reproduction or redistribution is strictly prohibited. All rights reserved.

Pollination of plants

Pollen can be carried to the female parts of other plants by wind or water. About 10% of pollination occurs this way. But most plants (80%) depend on animals for cross pollination. Many flowers produce fragrant smells and sweet nectar to attract bees, hummingbirds, other insects, and even certain kinds of bats. These animals feed on the nectar and pick up pollen on their bodies. Then when they fly to another plant the pollen is transferred to the female parts where fertilization takes place.

Cones vs. flowers in trees

Certain types of trees and shrubs called **conifers** produce pollen and seeds in **cones** instead of flowers. Pines, spruces, firs, and cypresses are examples of conifers. Their leaves look like pointed needles. The female cones that produce the seeds are much larger than the male cones. The conspicuous hard, woody, overlapping **bract scales** of the cones are modified leaves. Lying just above these are thin, flat **seed scales**. Each seed scale produces two **ovules**. When the ovules are fertilized by pollen from the male cones, they develop into seeds.

seeds are in here

Copyright © Mometrix Media. You have been licensed one copy of this document for personal use only. Any other reproduction or redistribution is strictly prohibited. All rights reserved.

Development of frogs

Frogs are **amphibians**. That means they must lay their eggs in water. The egg cell divides to form an **embryo** that grows until it begins to look like a **tadpole** (Fig. 1). Eventually the tadpole swims freely in the water and breathes with gills. As the tadpole develops it grows one hind leg (Fig. 2), then another (Fig. 3), and finally 2 front legs (Fig. 4). The tail shrinks (Fig. 5) until it disappears and the tadpole has **metamorphosed** into a tiny **frog**.

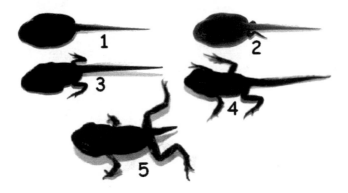

Metamorphosis

Nearly all insects undergo metamorphosis—a distinct change in form from their immature to adult stages. Many insects such as grasshoppers exhibit incomplete metamorphosis, in which the nymphs or juveniles resemble miniature adults but lack certain adult structures such as wings and genitalia. These insects undergo a series of growth stages known as instars, each of which is followed by a molt. Immature insects that exhibit complete metamorphosis are called larvae. At some point, these larvae spin a cocoon around themselves and become inactive pupae or chrysalides. After a time, they emerge as fully-formed adults. Butterflies, bees, and wasps are all examples of insects that undergo complete metamorphosis.

Development of butterflies

A butterfly egg hatches into a wormlike **caterpillar** (Fig. A). The caterpillar will shed its skin several times as it grows. When it is fully grown it will attach to a twig and shed its skin for the last time. Under this skin is a casing called a **chrysalis** (Fig. B). Inside this chrysalis the caterpillar has become a **pupa**. The pupa will **metamorphose** into an adult butterfly, which will crawl out of the chrysalis and wait for its wings to straighten out and dry (Fig. C).

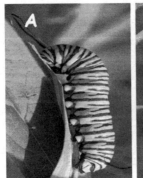

Copyright © Mometrix Media. You have been licensed one copy of this document for personal use only. Any other reproduction or redistribution is strictly prohibited. All rights reserved.

Competition between different organisms

Animals and plants have to compete with other species for food or nutrients, water, a place to live, nesting or breeding sites, sunlight in the case of plants, and other factors in the environment that may be scarce or limiting. Also, animals and plants of the same species have to compete with each other for the same things, as well in some cases for the right to breed and reproduce.

<u>Example of animals competing with each other</u>
Male elk known as bulls have large antlers, which they shed and regrow each year. Like their smaller deer cousins, bull elk engage in bugling contests and ritual combat (like the photo at right) to dominate other males and win all the female (cow) elk in a harem.

Plants competing for water

Creosote bush is the most widespread shrub in the deserts of the American Southwest where water can be very scarce for long periods. The roots of mature creosote bushes are extremely efficient and absorb all the water in the sandy soil around them. This creates very dry zones around each plant. The seeds of other plants cannot survive long enough to germinate. Therefore, the plants tend to be spaced far apart from each other as shown here.

Population of animals or plants

A population consists of all of the organisms of a certain kind in a defined area, region, or habitat. It may be all the red foxes in a given national park, all the loblolly pines in Virginia

Copyright © Mometrix Media. You have been licensed one copy of this document for personal use only. Any other reproduction or redistribution is strictly prohibited. All rights reserved.

(very hard to count), all the bullfrogs in a certain pond, or even all of the boxelder bugs on a single box elder tree. In the case of rare or endangered species it may be all of the individuals still living in the wild.

Nature controls the size of animal and plant populations

Several factors operate to keep animal and plant populations under control. Predation, grazing, disease, competition for limiting resources such as food or nutrients, water, habitat and living space, hunting and breeding territory, and sunlight for plants all play important roles. Even the size of the population can influence factors such as birth rate and severity of disease outbreaks or force individuals to migrate to other less crowded areas.

Hibernation

Hibernation occurs when an animal enters a state of inactivity in which its body temperature drops, and its breathing and metabolism slow down, and it goes into a deep sleep for many days, weeks, or even months. This allows animals to survive long, cold winters when food is scarce. Bears, ground squirrels and other rodents, some bats like the one shown hibernating here, and certain kinds of snakes are known to hibernate. Some animals sleep through hot summer weather or droughts. This is called **aestivation**.

Nocturnal animals

Nocturnal animals are active at night and sleep during the day. Nocturnal animals generally have very good senses of hearing and smell, and specially adapted eyes for seeing in the dark. Hunting or foraging for food at night is one way of avoiding competition for those resources from **diurnal** animals that are active during the day. Hawks and owls avoid competing with each other for prey in this way. Nocturnal animals also avoid the intense heat of the day in hot regions like deserts.

Ecology and ecosystems

Ecology is the study of the relationships between **organisms** (plants and animals) and their environment. The place where an organism lives is its habitat. Each organism must find everything it needs to live and reproduce within its habitat. Also within each habitat are other animals and plants as well as non-living factors such as soil, water, rocks, and nutrients. All of the organisms in a habitat make up the **community**, and the community combined with the non-living parts of the environment make up an **ecosystem**.

Copyright © Mometrix Media. You have been licensed one copy of this document for personal use only. Any other reproduction or redistribution is strictly prohibited. All rights reserved.

An ecosystem is a large or relatively small biological community, which consists of interacting groups of organisms of various species (plants, animals, fungi, etc.), as well as the physical environment, the climate, and the community's location in space and time. Each ecosystem has its characteristic groups of primary producers (photosynthesizers), primary and secondary consumers, predators, prey species, parasites, and decomposers. A community may be a small microcommunity of all the organisms in a single creosote bush or a vast assemblage of organisms in a biome spanning the better part of a continent. These biomes may include a tropical rain forest, temperate deciduous forest, taiga, grassland, chaparral, desert, tundra, or one of several major aquatic biomes. Regardless of its size, a given community will have numerous characteristic species.

Organisms adapting to their environment

Animals and plants are adapted to live in their environments in many special ways. For example, polar bears have white fur as camouflage which helps them blend in with their icy and snowy background. This makes it easier to sneak up on the seals on which they prey. They also have thick fur and a thick layer of blubber to help keep them warm in their frigid environment.

Camouflage vs. mimicry

Generally speaking, **camouflage** is when an organism blends in with its surroundings in a way that it cannot be seen as in the case of the flounder blending in with the gravel on the bottom of a lake (Fig. B). **Mimicry** is when an organism resembles something else, like the leaf insect in Fig. A. In these two examples each animal is able to avoid being seen and eaten by a predator. However, sometimes it is the predator that is camouflaged or a mimic which enables it to pounce on its unsuspecting prey.

Copyright © Mometrix Media. You have been licensed one copy of this document for personal use only. Any other reproduction or redistribution is strictly prohibited. All rights reserved.

Food web in a pond

Sunlight allows green algae to photosynthesize and grow. The algae are fed upon by small animals like water fleas and copepods. In turn, these are eaten by small worms, mosquito larvae and other larval insects. These are then eaten by mosquito fish, which in turn are eaten by larger fishes like bluegills. The bluegills are preyed upon by even larger fishes like bass and by herons, egrets and raccoons (which also eat the bass). Then the animal waste and everything that dies and settles to the bottom is decomposed by bacteria and fungi.

Food web in a typical meadow
Sunlight allows grass and other plants to grow. These plants are eaten by a variety of **herbivores** like insects, rodents, and rabbits. Their seeds are consumed by various birds such as sparrows and quail. The insects are eaten by **carnivores**, including other kinds of birds, shrews, and bats. The rodents, rabbits, and some of the birds are then eaten by larger carnivores like weasels and foxes. Also the quail, mice, rabbits and shrews are eaten by owls at night and by hawks during the day.

Predator vs. parasite

Predators are animals that attack and directly kill other animals for food. Lions, foxes, bats, snakes, hawks, and owls are examples of predators. **Parasites** are organisms that live on or inside another organism called a **host**. The parasite drains energy from the host and may release substances that harm it. Many parasites cause the host t to get sick and eventually may even kill it. However, with parasites the host is not killed outright as with predation. Bacteria, viruses, certain kinds of worms, mosquitoes, and ticks are examples of parasites.

Water cycle

The water cycle is the complex movement of water molecules in the form of liquid water, ice, and water vapor above, on, and within Earth, and from one area to another. Water can evaporate from the ocean to the atmosphere and condense out again as liquid rain, ice, or snow to fall on land, rivers, lakes, or the ocean. Water can be taken up by plant roots and transpired into the air from the leaves. The total amount of water on Earth remains roughly the same, but it constantly changes states (from liquid, to solid, to gas) as it moves from one place to another in the air, via ocean currents, or through other processes.

Copyright © Mometrix Media. You have been licensed one copy of this document for personal use only. Any other reproduction or redistribution is strictly prohibited. All rights reserved.

Water **evaporates** from plants, the soil, and open water as it is heated by the sun. As it rises this **water vapor** cools and **condenses** to form clouds and then **precipitates** (falls back to earth again) as rain, snow or hail. Some of this precipitation runs off into streams and rivers and eventually makes its way into lakes or the ocean. Some of it flows through the ground and is taken up by trees and other vegetation and the process begins all over again.

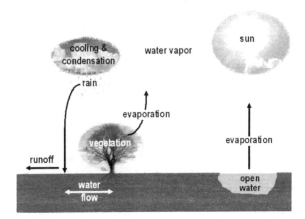

Animal migration

Many animals make a regular two-way, long-distance journey due to seasonal changes affecting the availability of food, weather or rainfall. Birds are especially noted for this, but other animals like bats, some butterflies, moths, and grasshoppers also migrate back and forth between northern winter and southern summer territories. Caribou and wildebeest also make spectacular migrations. The figure at right shows the 14,000-mile migration route of the Swainson's hawk, which spends its summers in western North America and winters in South America.

Precipitation

When the condensed water droplets or ice crystals forming in the cloud grow in size and become too heavy to stay aloft, they fall as rain, snowflakes, or hail.

Copyright © Mometrix Media. You have been licensed one copy of this document for personal use only. Any other reproduction or redistribution is strictly prohibited. All rights reserved.

Spider webs

Most spiders produce silk from glands at the tip of their abdomen. These glands can produce a trailing safety line and sticky silk making a web to trap their prey. An orb web like the one shown here lets the spider sit and wait for prey to be caught in the sticky web. This web helps the spider save energy since it does not have to hunt and chase down its prey like some spiders do. Weight for weight, spider silk is stronger than steel.

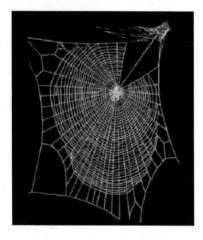

Insects

Insects are **arthropods** (joint-legged animals) whose bodies are divided into three parts: a head, thorax, and abdomen. Insects all have a hard outer covering called an **exoskeleton**, three pairs of legs (6 in all), compound eyes, and a single pair of antennae. They have to molt and shed their hard outer skin in order to grow. More than half of all living animals are insects. Spiders, scorpions, centipedes and millipedes are not insects but belong to different groups of arthropods.

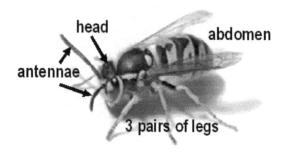

Copyright © Mometrix Media. You have been licensed one copy of this document for personal use only. Any other reproduction or redistribution is strictly prohibited. All rights reserved.

<u>Spiders and scorpions</u>

Spiders and scorpions are not insects, but arachnids. Spiders and scorpions have four pairs of walking legs, simple (not compound) eyes, and no antennae. The body is divided into two parts: a cephalothorax (the fused head and thorax) and an abdomen.

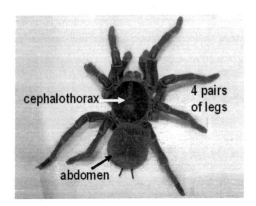

Warning coloration

Dangerously venomous or poisonous animals often are brightly colored to warn predators that they are best left alone. This is called aposematic coloration. The deadly venomous coral snake (Fig. A.) has bright red, yellow and black bands that circle its body. The harmless milk snake (Fig. B) mimics the dangerous coral snake which fools predators to leave them alone, too.

Instinctive behaviors

Instinctive behaviors are actions that are automatic in an animal and do not have to be taught or learned. Newly hatched sea turtles automatically crawl across the beach towards the ocean with no mother around to show them what to do. Tree squirrels automatically store acorns and nuts during the summer in order to have food in the coming winter. Also, salmon automatically return from the ocean to the freshwater river where they hatched in order to spawn.

Learned behaviors in animals

Many behaviors in higher animals such as birds and mammals actually have to be learned. Bird songs are usually learned. Male cardinals sing slightly different songs in different areas of the country. They learn these dialects from the adult birds around them. Also, unlike the instinctive migration of spawning salmon, sandhill cranes must be taught the long migration

Copyright © Mometrix Media. You have been licensed one copy of this document for personal use only. Any other reproduction or redistribution is strictly prohibited. All rights reserved.

routes they fly between their nesting and winter grounds. Likewise, most predatory mammals must learn how to hunt from their mothers.

Causes of weather

Heat energy from the sun warms different parts of the planet in different ways at different times. As warm air rises it expands and cools. This causes moisture to condense as liquid drops or freeze as ice crystals to form clouds. When the water drops or ice crystals become too large to stay aloft, they fall as precipitation. As warm air rises it also leaves a low pressure zone behind. This causes air from high surrounding high pressure zones to rush in as wind.

Photosynthesis

Green plants use energy from sunlight and carbon dioxide from the air to make sugars and energy-carrying molecules by **photosynthesis**. This word means "to put together with light." In this process plants give off oxygen as a waste product. This oxygen is then breathed in and used by animals.

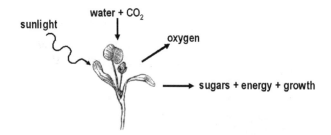

All of the oxygen in the atmosphere comes from photosynthesis by green plants, algae and some bacteria. The plants take in water and carbon dioxide and give off free oxygen as a waste product. Animals breathe in this oxygen and give off carbon dioxide and water as wastes, which are then used by the plants.

Photosynthesis is the process by which chlorophyll-containing autotrophs use the energy in sunlight to convert carbon dioxide and water into carbohydrates and release oxygen as a waste product. The general reaction is $2n\text{CO}_2 + 2n\text{H}_2\text{O} + h\nu$ (photons) $\rightarrow 2(\text{CH}_2\text{O})_n + 2n\text{O}_2$. The process involves two stages, which are known as the light and dark reactions. In the light reactions, photons provide the energy to split a water molecule. The electrons released are boosted into higher energy states and allowed to "flow downhill" (energetically speaking) to generate reducing equivalents—protons (H^+) and/or electrons (e^-)—and the energy-carrying molecule ATP. In the dark reactions, atmospheric CO_2 is captured and converted by the reducing equivalents and ATP into a 3-carbon sugar: PGAL. This PGAL is usually later converted into 6-carbon sugar phosphates, and then into sucrose, starch, and cellulose.

Copyright © Mometrix Media. You have been licensed one copy of this document for personal use only. Any other reproduction or redistribution is strictly prohibited. All rights reserved.

Animals and plants use of water, oxygen and carbon dioxide.

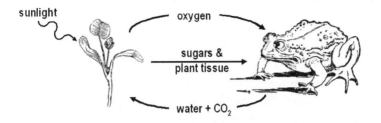

Rising and falling of the population of prey species

An example of this is the Canada lynx and snowshoe hare (a kind of rabbit) populations in the northern woods. Snowshoe hare populations rise and fall in cycles every 8 to 11 years. No one knows why. When hare populations rise, the lynx have more to eat and can raise more young. Therefore, the lynx populations also rise. Then when the hare populations fall, the lynxes also gradually die off or leave the area. Then the cycle repeats itself.

Physical properties between a glass of water and a five-gallon jug of water

The water in the glass and in the jug are exactly the same. There is no difference in the physical properties. Water is water regardless of the amount. Only the masses, weights, and volumes of the two containers of water are different. The chemical properties remain the same.

Shark vs. dolphin or porpoise

Sharks are a type of fish and breathe by means of gills. Although they look somewhat the same, dolphins and porpoises are mammals that live in the ocean. They breathe by means of lungs, and they must come to the surface to take in air through blowholes on top of their heads. Sharks swim by moving their vertical tails from side to side. Dolphins move their horizontal flukes up and down.

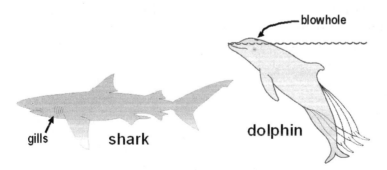

Producers, consumers, and decomposers

Producers are organisms that can make their own food. Most producers are plants. Through photosynthesis plants make sugars that provide energy. Plants only need sunlight, water, and the proper minerals and other nutrients to live, grow, and reproduce themselves. **Consumers** are organisms that eat other organisms. Consumers are animals that eat plants or other animals that eat plants. Decomposers are organisms that feed on decaying plant

Copyright © Mometrix Media. You have been licensed one copy of this document for personal use only. Any other reproduction or redistribution is strictly prohibited. All rights reserved.

and animal matter. Since decomposers cannot make their own food they are classified as consumers. Fungi such as mushrooms are **decomposers** that break down the tissues and wood of living or dead plants or the bodies of dead animals.

Mushrooms are fungi, and most are decomposers, which is a special type of consumer. Fungi have no chlorophyll and cannot engage in photosynthesis. Therefore, they cannot produce their own food and must get it from other organisms. Mushrooms are the fruiting bodies of fungi which live in the ground or grow the roots or trunks of living or dead trees. Mushrooms produce spores, which like the seeds of plants produce new fungal colonies. Some fungi are parasites on plants or animals or even other fungi.

Herbivores, carnivores and omnivores

Herbivores are animals that only eat plants. Examples are rabbits, deer, antelope, rhinoceroses and elephants. **Carnivores** are animals that only eat other animals, like lions, wolves, foxes, most bats, hawks and owls, insect-eating birds, snakes, and sharks. **Omnivores** are animals that eat both plants and other animals. Examples include bears, pigs, skunks, raccoons, birds like crows and ravens, and human beings.

Vultures

Vultures are mostly **scavenger**s that eat **carrion**— the dead and decaying flesh of animals. When an animal dies it immediately begins to decay or rot. Bacteria break down the dead tissues and release a foul smell that attracts scavengers like vultures, hyenas, crabs and lobsters, and certain flies that feed on decaying flesh. Many carnivores like coyotes, hyenas, opossums, hawks and eagles will also eat carrion in addition to catching live prey.

Formation of soils

Soils are formed when rock is broken down into smaller and smaller fragments by physical, chemical, and biological processes. This is called **weathering**. **Physical processes** include **erosion** and **transportation** by water and wind, freezing and thawing, and slumping due to gravity. **Chemical changes** alter the original substances present in rocks and early stage soils. **Biological processes** include burrowing by animals like earthworms and rodents and penetration by plant roots. As plants and animals die and decay, soils become rich in dark organic matter called **humus**.

Copyright © Mometrix Media. You have been licensed one copy of this document for personal use only. Any other reproduction or redistribution is strictly prohibited. All rights reserved.

Removal of vegetation from a habitat

When farmland is plowed repeatedly or a forest is completely cut down as in the photo at right, the soil is exposed to the actions of wind and rain. There is no covering of trees, bushes and grass, and the soil is no longer held together by dense tangles of roots. The soil is now washed away by rain and blown away by wind. Hillsides may be destroyed by landslides and slumping soil as shown here.

Jaws of a shark

The jaws of a great white shark are a very complex machine. The jaws form scissors, which is a complex machine made up of two wedges and a lever. Also, each tooth is a separate wedge, which means each jaw is a complex machine made up of many wedges. But it is even more complicated than that. Each tooth, as shown in the right-hand figure is a two-edged saw consisting of many tiny little teeth, each being a wedge. Therefore, this shark's jaws constitute a complex machine several times over.

Copyright © Mometrix Media. You have been licensed one copy of this document for personal use only. Any other reproduction or redistribution is strictly prohibited. All rights reserved.

Millipede

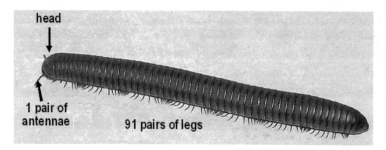

head

1 pair of antennae

91 pairs of legs

Millipedes are not insects. Millipedes and insects are both arthropods, but that is where the similarities end. Millipedes are called **myriapods**. Millipedes have 1 pair of antennae, but only simple eyes called **ocelli**. They have a head, a great many body segments, and **two pairs of legs** on most segments. Most eat dead plant matter. Insects have a pair of antennae, but they have compound eyes, a head, thorax, and abdomen, and just three pairs of legs.

Centipede

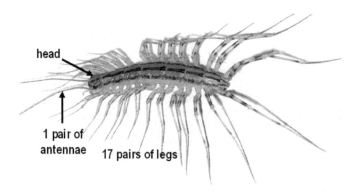

head

1 pair of antennae

17 pairs of legs

Centipedes are also not insects. They are called **chilopods**. They have a pair of antennae, many body segments, and **a single pair of legs** on each segment. Centipedes are carnivorous and have a pair of fangs formed from their first legs that they use to inject venom into their prey. Insects have a pair of antennae, but they have compound eyes, a head, thorax, and abdomen, and just three pairs of legs.

Copyright © Mometrix Media. You have been licensed one copy of this document for personal use only. Any other reproduction or redistribution is strictly prohibited. All rights reserved.

Vertebrates

A **vertebrate** is an animal with an internal **spinal column** (backbone) composed of soft cartilage or hard bone. Vertebrates also have a skull which contains a brain and most have paired **appendages** (legs, flippers or fins). Lampreys, sharks and rays, bony fishes, amphibians (frogs and salamanders), reptiles, birds and mammals are all vertebrates.

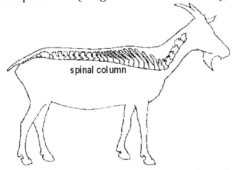

Image by Ruth Lawson Otago Polytechnic.

Adaptations observed in marine vertebrates

Sharks, porpoises, and extinct ichthyosaurs all separately and independently developed elongated, fusiform (spindle-shaped or torpedo-like) streamlined body forms, one or more erect dorsal fins, swimming flippers, and powerful swimming tails. All have somewhat similar outward appearances, but these animals are unrelated. Their similar appearance is the result of convergent evolution—the adaptive development of similar shapes in response to shared environments and predatory lifestyles. Sharks are cartilaginous fishes that breathe with gills, ichthyosaurs were air-breathing marine reptiles, and porpoises are air-breathing mammals whose ancestors lived on land.

Invertebrates

Invertebrates lack an internal spinal column. Their shape is maintained by a hard, rigid outer shell or covering called an exoskeleton or by the pressure of their internal fluids (like a plastic bag full of water). Insects, spiders, centipedes, snails, clams, octopuses and squids, and earthworms are all invertebrates.

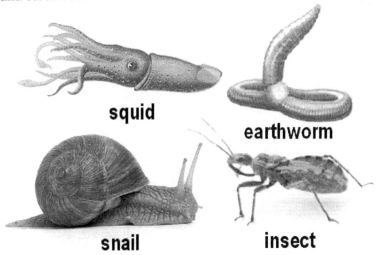

Copyright © Mometrix Media. You have been licensed one copy of this document for personal use only. Any other reproduction or redistribution is strictly prohibited. All rights reserved.

Mammal

Mammals are air-breathing, warm-blooded vertebrates with a backbone, skull, internal skeleton and a well-developed brain. Most are covered with hair, and most have specialized teeth. Most give birth to live young, and the mothers produce milk to nourish their young. Birds are also warm-blooded, but they are covered with feathers instead of hair, their young hatch from hard-shelled eggs, and they have no teeth. Bats, platypuses, opossums, kangaroos, elephants, deer, squirrels, apes, monkeys, and whales are all mammals.

Reptile

Reptiles are air-breathing vertebrates. They cannot generate their own body heat like mammals and birds. Their skin is covered with scales or horny plates. Some lay eggs on land, and others have eggs that hatch inside the mother, and the young are born live. Crocodiles and alligators, turtles, lizards and snakes (like the cobra shown here) are all reptiles. Other reptiles include the dinosaurs, ichthyosaurs, and flying reptiles that died out millions of years ago.

Copyright © Mometrix Media. You have been licensed one copy of this document for personal use only. Any other reproduction or redistribution is strictly prohibited. All rights reserved.

Amphibian

Amphibians are cold-blooded, air-breathing vertebrates with a smooth and slimy or dry and warty skin. Most lay their eggs in water, but a few lay eggs in wet areas on land. Unlike reptiles and birds, amphibian eggs lack any kind of protective outer shell. Many amphibians undergo metamorphosis from a gill-breathing tadpole stage to an air-breathing adult. Frogs, toads, and salamanders are all amphibians.

toad

salamander

Fish

Except for lungfish, fishes are gill-breathing animals with a backbone, skull and internal skeleton that live in the water (although some can come out on land for short periods). They have no legs, but most have paired fins for swimming. Most are cold-blooded, although a few fast swimmers can raise their body temperature slightly. They lay their eggs in the water. Sharks, bass, tuna, salmon, goldfish, and catfish are all different types of fishes.

Innate (instinctive) vs. learned behavior

Innate, or instinctive, behavior includes actions that are programmed by an animal's genes. It is behavior that is elicited automatically in response to environmental or social cues. It is not based on prior experience or learning. Examples include marine turtle hatchlings automatically moving toward the ocean and safety. Learned behavior must be taught by more experienced mentors; it is acquired through learning. Examples include many territorial songs sung by male songbirds, which must be taught. Different populations of the same species of songbird sing slightly different songs (dialects). Similarly, in the 1930s and 1940s in England, birds known as Great Tits learned to open milk bottles that were delivered to people's doorsteps and drink the milk. This behavior was learned and passed along by inexperienced birds watching experienced birds, and the behavior spread quickly throughout the country. Likewise, bears in national parks have learned to associate humans with food, which has caused major conflicts and problems in these areas.

Plate tectonics

Earthquakes result from the movement of a dozen or so major lithospheric (crustal) plates that float upon Earth's mantle (asthenosphere). These plates move about each other in

Copyright © Mometrix Media. You have been licensed one copy of this document for personal use only. Any other reproduction or redistribution is strictly prohibited. All rights reserved.

response to complex convection cells set in motion by Earth's interior heat. Two plates move apart from each other at divergent boundaries, or spreading centers, and come together at convergent boundaries. When thin, denser, iron- and magnesium- rich oceanic crust collides with thicker, lighter, silica-rich continental crust, the former is subducted beneath the latter. The subducted material carries scraped-off continental crust and seawater down with it. As this material melts, it rises as a mixture of magma and steam to produce explosive volcanic mountain ranges such as those surrounding the Pacific Ocean Basin. When two continental plates collide at convergent boundaries, the crust buckles and thrusts up massive mountain ranges such as the Alps and Himalayas.

Significance of fossils

Fossils are the preserved traces, casts, or mineralized remains of animals, plants, and other organisms that lived tens of thousands, millions, or even billions of years ago. Preserved remains younger than about 10,000 years are not generally considered fossils, but there is no particularly good reason for this other than convention. Most fossils are mineralized hard parts such as teeth, bones, and shells that were buried. The organic material was gradually replaced, molecule by molecule, with minerals. Therefore, the structural details are preserved. In some cases, soft objects such as feathers and leaves and delicate creatures such as insects and spiders were buried in mud, where their detailed casts were preserved. They may also have been trapped in tree sap and fossilized intact in amber. The sedimentary environments and strata in which fossils are found reveal a great deal about the habitats and environments of the preserved plants and organisms. Many fossils can be accurately dated by radiometric means.

Copyright © Mometrix Media. You have been licensed one copy of this document for personal use only. Any other reproduction or redistribution is strictly prohibited. All rights reserved.

Earth Sciences

Solar system

The **solar sy**stem consists of the sun and eight **major planets**. In order from the sun the planets are Mercury, Venus, Earth, Mars, Jupiter, Saturn, Uranus and Neptune. Pluto is no longer considered to be a major planet. Along with 5 other similar sized objects it is now a **minor pla**net. Six of the major planets have one or more moons. The solar system also contains countless **meteoroids**, **asteroid**s, and **comet**s.

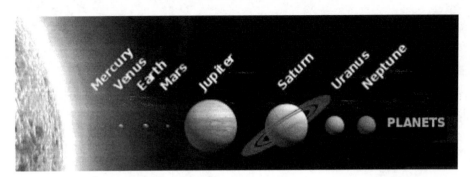

Major bodies in our Solar System

Our solar system consists of the Sun and the eight major planets that orbit it. Arranged in order from the closest to the farthest from the Sun, these planets are: Mercury, Venus, Earth, Mars, Jupiter, Saturn, Uranus, and Neptune. Between Mars and Jupiter lies the asteroid belt of small, rocky objects of varying sizes. Pluto is no longer considered a planet, and is now classified as one of the five known trans-Neptunian objects regarded as minor planets. The Kuiper Belt extends from Neptune at 30 astronomical units [1 AU (the mean distance from the Sun to Earth) is 150 million km] out to about 50 AU, or 1 light-year (~9.5 trillion kilometers) from the Sun. It contains countless numbers of icy bodies of water, methane, and ammonia, some with rocky cores. Beyond the Kuiper Belt lies the hypothesized spherical Oort Cloud, thought to be the source of long-period comets.

Life cycle of a star

Stars are formed when enormous clouds of interstellar molecular gas (primarily hydrogen and helium) and dust collapse under their own gravitational attraction. As the molecular cloud collapses, its pressure increases and it heats up to form an ionized gas (plasma). Eventually, it will reach core temperatures of between 4 million kelvins (K) for a small star and 40 million K for a massive star. These temperatures drive hydrogen atoms together so that they fuse and form helium. Some of the matter contained in the four hydrogen atoms is lost as energy, which prevents further gravitational collapse of the star. Depending on its mass, the star will continue to shine for several million years (very massive stars) to 10 billion years (our Sun) or even longer. Most stars will go on to form other elements later in their life cycle until they begin to synthesize iron. At that point no energy is released and, depending on its remaining mass, the star will collapse into a white dwarf, a neutron star, or a black hole.

Copyright © Mometrix Media. You have been licensed one copy of this document for personal use only. Any other reproduction or redistribution is strictly prohibited. All rights reserved.

Milky Way

On a clear dark moonless night far from city lights a broad white band of stars that stretches across the sky can be seen. This is the Milky Way galaxy, and our sun and the solar system are part of it. The Milky Way is a huge flat disk containing between 200 billion and 400 billion stars. Because Earth is in that disk, we see it edge on, which is why it appears to us as a broad band of light.

The Milky Way is a flat, disk-shaped spiral galaxy with a central bar-like bulge of stars. It is huge—between 100,000 and 120,000 light-years in diameter. A light-year is a unit of distance, not time. It is the distance light travels in one year, about 6 trillion miles. The Milky Way is between 600 thousand trillion and 700 thousand trillion miles across. Our solar system lies about two thirds of the way out on one of the spiral arms.

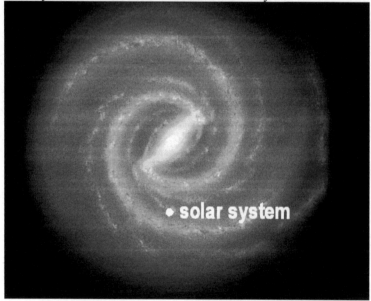

The Milky Way galaxy is a giant spiral galaxy some 100,000 light-years (ly), or about 9.46×10^{17} kilometers ($\sim$946 thousand trillion km) in diameter. Recent evidence suggests that the Milky Way has a central bar and may have to be reclassified as a "barred spiral" or intermediate type galaxy. It contains about 200 billion stars and is one of at least 200 billion galaxies in the known Universe. It is home to our Sun and its solar system, located about

Copyright © Mometrix Media. You have been licensed one copy of this document for personal use only. Any other reproduction or redistribution is strictly prohibited. All rights reserved.

26,000 light-years (~246 thousand trillion km, or a little over halfway out) from the galactic center on the inner edge of the Orion-Cygnus arm. Like the galaxy's size, the exact distance is not precisely known because of clouds of gas and dust that obscure our view from Earth. Our solar system revolves around the center of the galaxy approximately once every 250 million years.

Seasons on Earth

Earth is tilted on its axis as it revolves around the Sun and rotates upon its axis from left to right. That means more sunshine and longer days and shorter nights in the hemisphere facing the Sun. More sunlight means warmer temperatures. In the left-hand picture the Southern Hemisphere is experiencing its summer. Six months later when Earth is on the opposite side of the Sun (right-hand picture), it is the Northern Hemisphere that is having summer.

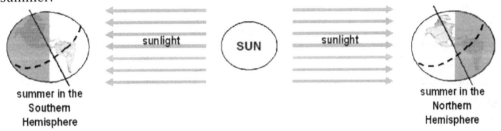

summer in the Southern Hemisphere

summer in the Northern Hemisphere

Relationships between Earth, the Moon, and the Sun

Earth is the third planet from the Sun. It orbits the Sun once every 365.256 days. A solar year is therefore 6 hours longer than 365 days, which is why an extra day is added to the calendar year every four years. In a leap year, February has an extra day and the year is 366 days long. Earth rotates on its axis approximately once every 24 hours, constituting a day. The Moon rotates in synch with Earth, meaning it turns on its axis once in the time it takes to orbit Earth. Therefore, the same side of the Moon is always visible to viewers on Earth; humans did not see the far side of the Moon until manned spacecraft orbited it.

Copyright © Mometrix Media. You have been licensed one copy of this document for personal use only. Any other reproduction or redistribution is strictly prohibited. All rights reserved.

Rising and setting of the Sun

Earth rotates on its axis from west to east as it orbits around the Sun. This means that people in the East are the first to see the Sun as it rises, while those in the West are the last to see it as it sets.

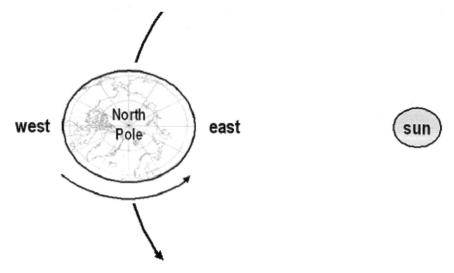

Earth vs. moon

The diameter of the Moon is slightly more than one quarter that of Earth. The average distance between them is about 385,000 kilometers (60 times the radius of Earth), although it varies from approximately 362,500 (356,400–370,400) kilometers at perigee (its closest approach) to about 405,400 (404,000–406,700) kilometers at apogee (its farthest distance from Earth). If Earth were the size of a quarter, the Moon would be about 6¼ feet (1.9 meters) away. The following graphic shows the relative sizes of Earth and the Moon and their average distance from each other.

Copyright © Mometrix Media. You have been licensed one copy of this document for personal use only. Any other reproduction or redistribution is strictly prohibited. All rights reserved.

Phases of the Moon

As the moon revolves around Earth approximately every 27.3 days, light from the Sun hits it from different angles. This causes the Moon to be in full sunlight (full moon) when Earth is between it and the Sun, complete darkness (new moon) when it is between Earth and the Sun, and all stages in between. When the Moon is half in sunlight and half in shadow it is in the first or last quarter, depending on whether it is heading towards becoming a full moon or a new moon.

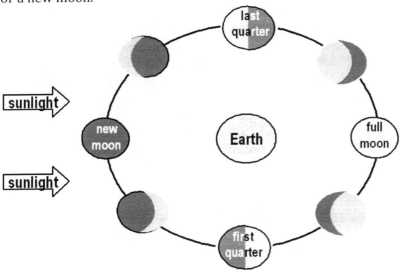

Earth's atmosphere

Earth's gravity is strong enough to attract the molecules of the gases in the atmosphere and keep them in a layer surrounding the planet. The gravity of smaller celestial bodies like Mercury and Earth's moon is not strong enough to do this, and their atmospheres long ago diffused out into space.

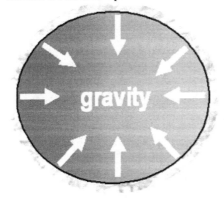

Climate vs. weather

Climate refers to the more or less stable, usually regional (as opposed to worldwide) statistical patterns of temperature; humidity; type (rainfall, snow, ice) and timing of precipitation; amount of frost, sunshine, and clouds; prevalence, direction, and speed of winds; seasonal patterns (including the prevalence and types of storms and severe weather); and other atmospheric and meteorological phenomena over many decades to

Copyright © Mometrix Media. You have been licensed one copy of this document for personal use only. Any other reproduction or redistribution is strictly prohibited. All rights reserved.

hundreds, thousands, or even millions of years. Climate is influenced by latitude and longitude, altitude, geography, and the presence of nearby mountain ranges or large bodies of water such as the Great Lakes or oceans. Climate can also apply to the planet as a whole when referring to time periods such as glacial epochs ("ice ages"). Conversely, weather is the short-term (days, weeks, months) variation in meteorological conditions in a given region.

Geological weathering and erosion

All rocks, minerals, and soils are subject to the forces of weathering and erosion. Weathering is the mechanical and/or chemical breakdown of rock by liquid water, wind, ice, snow, temperature changes, and the biological actions of organisms. Erosion involves the breakdown, movement, and transportation of parent rock and soil by water, wind, ice, or simple gravity. Water erodes bedrock by both mechanical and chemical processes: alternate freezing and thawing cracks rocks (frost wedging or frost heaving), carbonic acid formed by CO_2 dissolved in water chemically dissolves limestone and other susceptible rocks, and salts and other minerals may precipitate out as new minerals. Mass wasting involves the downslope movement of soil and rocks due to gravity. Lichens and mosses create a humid environment and also directly attack rocks chemically, and many burrowing and tunneling organisms hasten the breakdown of soil.

Clouds

Clouds form when water vapor in the atmosphere cools to the point where it condenses out as water droplets or small particles of frozen ice crystals that we can see. Clouds can also form when more moisture is added to the air by evaporation until the air becomes saturated and cannot hold any more water. Then the water vapor will begin to condense into visible droplets.

Copyright © Mometrix Media. You have been licensed one copy of this document for personal use only. Any other reproduction or redistribution is strictly prohibited. All rights reserved.

Tornado

A tornado is a violent rotating column of air that is in contact with both the ground and a cloud. The column is visible because the very low pressure causes water vapor to condense out as visible water droplets. Where the tornado touches the ground it usually stirs up a cloud of dirt and debris like the one in this photo. Tornadoes are the most violent storms on Earth, and the strongest spin at 300 miles per hour.

Conditions inside a tornado.

A tornado is a violent rotating column of air usually extending from a severe thunderstorm to contact Earth's surface on either land or water. Tornadoes can occur almost anywhere in the world (except Antarctica), but the most common and dangerous ones occur in the United States between the Rocky Mountains and Appalachian Mountains in an area nicknamed "Tornado Alley". The rotating column of air is invisible until a funnel forms from condensed water droplets and/or dust and debris from the ground. The extreme rotating wind speeds reduce pressure inside the funnel significantly (Bernoulli's principle). The expanding air molecules inside this low-pressure vortex perform work causing the temperature to drop until water vapor condenses into visible droplets, forming a condensation funnel. An F0 tornado on the Fujita scale has wind speeds of 64–116 km/h (40–72 mph) and cause minimal damage. The most violent F5 tornados can have wind speeds over 500 km/h (310 mph) and cause catastrophic damage and loss of life. Fortunately, F5 tornadoes are rare.

Copyright © Mometrix Media. You have been licensed one copy of this document for personal use only. Any other reproduction or redistribution is strictly prohibited. All rights reserved.

Hurricanes

A hurricane is a very large tropical storm that forms over the open ocean and produces very strong winds and heavy rains. A tropical storm forms when warm water evaporates and the saturated air rises and forms a column of condensed water vapor. As the wind speed increases the pressure falls even more and a hurricane can be born. Sinking air in the center of the storm produces an eye (arrow) where the weather is quite calm and free of clouds.

Lightning bolt

Lightning is a huge electric spark that can occur inside a cloud, go from one cloud to another, or go from a cloud to the ground. The turbulent rising air and rising and falling raindrops or ice crystals in a thunderstorm cause differences in electric charge in different parts of the cloud and between the bottom of the cloud and the ground. When the difference in charge is large enough, a lightning bolt will discharge which neutralizes the difference.

Copyright © Mometrix Media. You have been licensed one copy of this document for personal use only. Any other reproduction or redistribution is strictly prohibited. All rights reserved.

Thunder

As a lightning bolt travels through the air, it pushes the air aside faster than the speed of sound. This produces a shock wave of very hot air that creates a loud sonic boom, which we hear as thunder. If a person can hear thunder, he needs to get indoors quickly as possible since he could be struck by lightning.

We hear thunder later because sound travels much slower than light. Light travels so fast that it is almost instantaneous from one point to another anywhere on Earth. Sound travels much more slowly—about one mile every five seconds or so. Light would travel one mile in only about 5 millionths of a second. Therefore, the distance from a lightning flash can be determined by counting the number of seconds until the thunder it made is heard.

Causes of earthquakes

Earthquakes result when an amount of energy large enough to cause a noticeable movement of the ground is suddenly released. This can be due to sudden slippage along faults, crustal plate boundaries, or at mid-oceanic seafloor spreading zones when the accumulated stress (potential energy) from plate tectonic movement is suddenly released as kinetic energy. A combination of upwelling convection currents in the mantle at seafloor spreading zones and tensile forces pulling the plates apart under their own weight at subduction zones cause oceanic plates to move relative to one another. This in turn causes collateral stresses along faults and other zones of lithospheric weakness. Large sections of crust become locked in place because of friction as the stresses accumulate. When the accumulated stress is sufficient to overcome this friction, a sudden slippage occurs, generating earthquakes. Earthquakes can also be caused by volcanic activity, massive landslides, nuclear explosions, and other events.

Comet

Comets are small icy bodies ranging in size from tens of yards to tens of miles in diameter. They orbit the sun with periods of a few years to hundreds of thousands of years. Halley's comet shown here orbits the sun every 75 to 76 years. As a comet nears the sun a long tail or coma is created as ice and dust are blown off by the intense radiation and the solar wind of charged particles from the sun.

Copyright © Mometrix Media. You have been licensed one copy of this document for personal use only. Any other reproduction or redistribution is strictly prohibited. All rights reserved.

Meteoroids and meteors

A **meteoroid** is a sand- to boulder-sized piece of debris hurtling through the solar system at speeds of between 15 and 45 miles per second. When it enters earth's atmosphere it burns up and leaves a visible fiery trail of gas and debris called a **meteor**. Some meteoroids are large enough that they do not completely burn up, and what remains reaches the ground. These are called **meteorites**. Meteoroids can be small pieces that have broken off of **asteroids**.

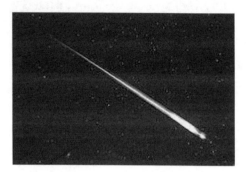

Dew

During the night the cooler air causes water vapor to condense into water drops on the surfaces of objects. As the sun heats up the air later in the morning, these water drops evaporate again into water vapor. The amount of moisture air can hold as water vapor depends on its temperature. Warm air can hold more water vapor than cool or cold air.

Carbon dioxide-oxygen cycle

Photosynthetic plants and algae take in carbon dioxide (CO_2) from the air, which is converted into 3-carbon sugar compounds. During photosynthesis, a water molecule (H_2O) is split, and oxygen gas (O_2) is given off as a waste product. Animals, plants, fungi, algae, and other organisms that engage in cellular respiration break down the sugars produced by photosynthesis and use the oxygen produced by green plants to produce energy in the form of ATP molecules. In addition to energy, cellular respiration produces O_2 and H_2O as waste products, which are then used by primary producers (photosynthetic organisms) to produce sugars.

Potential vs. kinetic energy

Potential energy is stored energy that can be released to do work. Kinetic energy is "energy in motion" that actively performs work within or against a system. For example, if you carry a basketball up a flight of stairs against the force of gravity, you have stored that gravitational energy in the ball as potential energy. If you then let the ball bounce down the stairs, that energy is released as kinetic energy, which can knock over a glass of milk or other object that happens to be in its way.

Flow of solar energy through ecosystems

About 30 percent of the total energy from the Sun that reaches the Earth is reflected back into space. Of the remaining 70 percent, one-third is absorbed by clouds and two-thirds

- 44 -

Copyright © Mometrix Media. You have been licensed one copy of this document for personal use only. Any other reproduction or redistribution is strictly prohibited. All rights reserved.

make it to Earth's surface (land and water), where it drives weather patterns and ocean currents. Most of this energy is ultimately radiated back into space. Less than 1 percent is actually available to be used by plants and other primary producers for photosynthesis. Of the solar energy that reaches the producers, 90 percent is lost as heat, and only about 1 percent is used to produce sugars. Animals that eat plants use only about 1 percent of the energy they consume; the rest is lost as heat. Likewise, predators feeding on primary consumers and decomposers can only absorb and use 1 percent of the energy they take in. The number of steps in this chain must be limited for there to be sufficient solar energy to sustain life.

Renewable and nonrenewable resources

Renewable sources of energy include solar, wind, tidal, and geothermal resources. These can be tapped essentially without limit. Nonrenewable energy resources include coal, oil, natural gas, and other "fossil fuels." Once these are mined they cannot be replaced. Minerals are not renewable, at least not on a time scale that works for human societies. Timber harvested for lumber, wild fish stocks, and aquatic food resources other than fish are renewable if they are properly managed and not overexploited to the point that they cannot replace themselves.

Igneous, sedimentary, and metamorphic rocks

Igneous rock forms when hot magma or lava cools beneath or above the ground, respectively, to form large- or fine-grained crystalline, porous, or glassy rocks of varying chemical compositions. Sedimentary rocks form from previously weathered (eroded) parent rock, which itself may be igneous, sedimentary, or metamorphic. This weathered material deposits out in layers and eventually becomes compacted and/or chemically solidified into sedimentary rock. Sedimentary rocks can also form as coal or as limestone or dolomite from the heating and compaction of calcareous exoskeletons of aquatic animals and algae. Sediments can also form as salt deposits from evaporating water bodies. Metamorphic rocks are altered, partially re-melted, and generally highly crystalline igneous, sedimentary, or even older metamorphic rocks that have undergone various degrees of heating and compression. Heat from volcanic sills and dikes can produce contact metamorphism in immediately adjacent rock, while uplifting mountain ranges result in large-scale regional metamorphism.

Formation of deltas, canyons, and dunes

A delta is landform that is created at the mouth of a river, where it flows into a larger body of water. The river carries sediment and when it reaches the larger body of water it spreads out and deposits the sediment. An example would be the Mississippi Delta, where the Mississippi River meets the Gulf of Mexico. A canyon is a deep ravine between two cliffs. It is usually formed by the erosion of flowing water over extended periods of time. A famous example of this is the Grand Canyon in Arizona. A sand dune is a mound of sand built by natural forces, usually wind, over time. Great Sand Dunes National Park, located in Colorado, is home to the tallest sand dunes in the United States.

Copyright © Mometrix Media. You have been licensed one copy of this document for personal use only. Any other reproduction or redistribution is strictly prohibited. All rights reserved.

Weather maps, symbols, and key

A weather map is a map that shows the weather and other meteorological features of a given region at a particular time. Weather maps contain various symbols or shaded regions that have specific meanings and indicate certain weather patterns or events. They include indicators for precipitation, wind, fog, high/low pressure areas, and temperature. A map key may be included to give a brief description of what each item on the map indicates. Modern media also allow for the rapid cycling of weather maps across a range of time to give a moving picture of the weather over a period of hours or days.

Changes in tides, seasons, and the appearance of the Moon

The tide is the changing level of water in a large body of water such as a lake or an ocean. This change in water level is shown by how far the water comes up on the land. When the water level is high, a time known as high tide, the water comes up farther onto the shoreline. At low tide, the water level is lower, and the water recedes. Tides are primarily caused by the gravitational pull of the moon. The year is divided up into four seasons: spring, summer, fall (or autumn), and winter. Each season has particular meteorological and ecological characteristics for which it is known. For instance, spring is known as the time in which plants begin to bloom after being dormant for the cold winter. The days are longer in the summer when the earth's tilt affords it a longer period of sunlight. Most of the features of each season can be attributed to the orientation of the earth in its yearly orbit around the sun. The appearance of the moon from the earth varies from just a sliver of white to a bright full circle, depending on where the moon is in its orbit about the earth. The moon orbits the earth every 29.5 days. Half of the moon is always lit by the sun (except in the case of a lunar eclipse), but the moon's position in its orbit determines how much of that half is visible from the earth.

Copyright © Mometrix Media. You have been licensed one copy of this document for personal use only. Any other reproduction or redistribution is strictly prohibited. All rights reserved.

Investigation And Experimentation

English and metric (scientific) units of measurement

The English system commonly used in the United States is not based on consistent smaller units. Thus, 12 inches equal 1 foot, 3 feet equal 1 yard, and 5,280 feet equal 1 mile. The metric system used in science and most countries of the world is based on units of 10. Therefore, 1000 millimeters and 100 centimeters equal 1 meter, and 1,000 meters equal a kilometer. The same pattern is true for the other units of measurement in the two systems. The following table shows the different units.

unit	English system	Metric system
length	inch, foot, mile	centimeter, meter, kilometer
mass, weight	net weight ounce, pound	gram, kilogram, newton
volume	fluid ounce, pint, quart	milliliter, liter
temperature	Fahrenheit degree	Celsius degree

Fahrenheit and Celsius temperature scales

In the Fahrenheit scale the point where water freezes and ice melts is set at 32°, and the point where water boils and water vapor condenses is 212°. That means a difference of 180° between the freezing and boiling points of water. In the Celsius scale, the freezing/melting point is set at 0°and the boiling/condensation point at 100°, making this scale much easier to use.

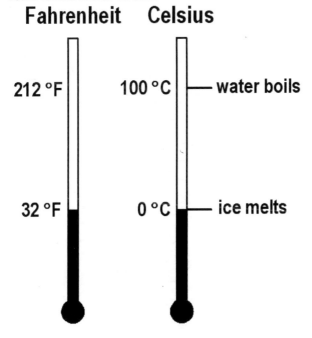

Copyright © Mometrix Media. You have been licensed one copy of this document for personal use only. Any other reproduction or redistribution is strictly prohibited. All rights reserved.

Different states of water

On a cold day breathe into a glass jar with a screw-on lid until droplets of water from your breath condense (change from a gas to a liquid) onto the inside of the jar. Then screw the lid down and put the jar in a warm window or other warm spot. As the air inside the jar warms, the water droplets will evaporate into an invisible gas and will disappear. Now cool the jar down again (perhaps outside in the cold) and watch as the water droplets form again.

Scientific method

Scientists investigate natural phenomena by completing the following steps: (1) making observations and recording facts and data, (2) formulating a hypothesis or plausible explanation for the data, (3) making one or more predictions based on the hypothesis about what might happen (if x is true, then y must follow), (4) conducting one or more experiments to test whether the hypothesis holds up or must be rejected, and (5) forming a conclusion based on the experimental outcome. To be credible, hypotheses must be consistent with the rest of scientific knowledge. No limit exists as to the creativity that may be involved in a scientific investigation. However, most experiments involve a test, experimental group of things, or organism, as well as a single variable to be tested. There is also a control group, which is treated exactly the same as the test group; the only thing that is altered is the single variable being studied. If the experiment fails to support the hypothesis, it must be at least provisionally rejected.

Copyright © Mometrix Media. You have been licensed one copy of this document for personal use only. Any other reproduction or redistribution is strictly prohibited. All rights reserved.

Practice Test #1

Practice Questions

1. In a science experiment, a student is asked to identify the freezing and melting points of water. Which piece of laboratory equipment should be used?

Ⓐ Balance

Ⓑ Thermometer

Ⓒ Ruler

Ⓓ Graduated cylinder

2. In the diagram shown below, four wheels are in contact such that each wheel turns the opposite direction from the wheels it is touching. Wheel A is being turned clockwise by a force as shown. Which statement about wheel D is correct?

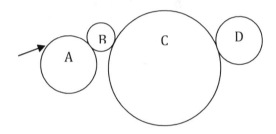

Ⓐ Wheel D does not turn at all because there are too many wheels between it and wheel A

Ⓑ Wheel D does not turn at all because it is not touching wheel C

Ⓒ Wheel D turns counterclockwise

Ⓓ Wheel D turns clockwise

3. The United States is divided into four time zones. The east coast is three hours ahead of the west coast. This means that when it is 6:00pm in New York, on the east coast, it is 3:00pm in California on the west coast. Based on the information given, which direction does Earth rotate on its axis?

Ⓐ Clockwise as viewed from above the north pole

Ⓑ Counterclockwise as viewed from above the north pole

Ⓒ Toward the Sun

Ⓓ The direction varies depending on the season

Copyright © Mometrix Media. You have been licensed one copy of this document for personal use only. Any other reproduction or redistribution is strictly prohibited. All rights reserved.

4. A boy is outside in the winter and notices that he begins shivering when he gets cold. A girl is outside during the summer and begins sweating when she gets hot. Why do the children's bodies react this way?

Ⓐ The children's bodies are attempting to regulate their temperature

Ⓑ The children's bodies are trying to fight off disease

Ⓒ The children's bodies are reacting to the amount of sunlight or shade

Ⓓ The children are having an allergic reaction to something in the air

5. How does the tilt of Earth's axis cause seasons?

Ⓐ A hemisphere experiences winter when that half of Earth is tilted away from the Sun. It experiences summer when that half of Earth is tilted towards the Sun

Ⓑ A hemisphere experiences spring when that half of Earth is tilted away from the Sun. It experiences autumn when that half of Earth is tilted towards the Sun

Ⓒ A hemisphere experiences summer when that half of Earth is tilted away from the Sun. It experiences winter when that half of Earth is tilted towards the Sun

Ⓓ A hemisphere experiences autumn when that half of Earth is tilted away from the Sun. It experiences spring when that half of Earth is tilted towards the Sun

Power Fruit
All natural fruit juice that gives you energy all day long
35 mg of caffeine
50% daily value of Vitamin E
100% daily value of Vitamin C

6. The advertisement above shows the nutrition information for the new juice, "Power Fruit". Which conclusion can be made about Power Fruit?

Ⓐ Power Fruit contains the daily value of caffeine

Ⓑ Power Fruit provides all the vitamin C you need each day

Ⓒ Power Fruit has 100% daily value of vitamin A

Ⓓ Power Fruit does not contain iron

Copyright © Mometrix Media. You have been licensed one copy of this document for personal use only. Any other reproduction or redistribution is strictly prohibited. All rights reserved.

7. Which of the following sources of fresh water is unavailable for human use?

Ⓐ Rivers

Ⓑ Estuaries

Ⓒ Aquifers

Ⓓ Glaciers

8. How are igneous rocks formed?

Ⓐ Years of sediment are laid down on top of each other and forced together

Ⓑ Acid rain caused by pollution creates holes in metamorphic rocks

Ⓒ Dust and pebbles are pressed together underground from Earth's heat and pressure

Ⓓ Magma from a volcanic eruption cools and hardens

9. Jim and John are working on their science fair project when they accidently break a beaker. What should the boys do?

Ⓐ Tell their teacher immediately

Ⓑ Clean up the broken glass themselves

Ⓒ Move away from the broken glass and continue working

Ⓓ Hide the broken glass so they don't get in trouble

10. Why do balloons filled with helium float while balloons filled with air do not float?

Ⓐ Balloons filled with air are larger than balloons filled with helium, which makes them heavier preventing them from floating

Ⓑ Helium is less dense than air, which allows balloons filled with helium to float

Ⓒ Helium balloons travel on higher air currents and balloons filled with air travel on lower air currents

Ⓓ Air causes balloons to generate static electricity so the balloon will be attracted to the ground

11. Which of the following is the most likely food source for a carnivore?

Ⓐ A plant

Ⓑ The Sun

Ⓒ An animal

Ⓓ A dead tree

Copyright © Mometrix Media. You have been licensed one copy of this document for personal use only. Any other reproduction or redistribution is strictly prohibited. All rights reserved.

12. Why are plants considered producers?

Ⓐ They make their own food

Ⓑ They soak up water from the ground

Ⓒ Their leaves can be large or small

Ⓓ They produce pollen, which is a food source for many insects and birds

13. How should students determine the volume of fluid in a graduated cylinder?

Ⓐ Read the volume at the bottom of the meniscus

Ⓑ Read the volume at the highest point the fluid reaches

Ⓒ Read the volume at the center, between the meniscus and the highest point of the fluid

Ⓓ Read the volume at the highest point then round to the nearest tens

14. A student is conducting an experiment using a ball that is attached to the end of a string on a pendulum. The student pulls the ball back so that it is at an angle to its resting position. As the student releases the ball, it swings forward and backward. The student measures the time it takes the ball to make one complete period. A period is defined as the time it takes the ball to swing forward and back again to its starting position. This is repeated using different string lengths.

The student formed the following hypothesis: *Lengthening the string of the pendulum increases the time it takes the ball to make one complete period.*

What correction would you have the student make to the hypothesis?

Ⓐ Turn it into an "if/then" statement

Ⓑ Add the word "will" in the middle after the word "pendulum"

Ⓒ Switch the order of the sentence so that the phrase about the period comes first, and the phrase about the string's length is last

Ⓓ No corrections are needed

Copyright © Mometrix Media. You have been licensed one copy of this document for personal use only. Any other reproduction or redistribution is strictly prohibited. All rights reserved.

15. When should instructions for a laboratory experiment be read?

(A) Instructions only need to be read if the teacher does not explain the steps of the lab well

(B) The instructions should be read if the students get confused or are not sure of the steps in the lab

(C) Instructions should be read thoroughly before beginning the lab

(D) The instructions do not need to be read, they are only a suggestion for how to complete the lab

16. A ball is thrown and the distance it traveled is measured. Which data set corresponds to the graph below?

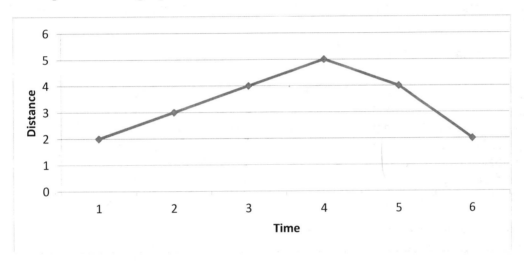

(A)

Time	Distance
1	2
2	4
3	6
4	8
5	9

(C)

Time	Distance
2	0
4	1
6	3
8	5
9	7

(B)

Time	Distance
1	2
3	4
5	6
7	8
9	9

(D)

Time	Distance
1	2
2	3
3	4
4	5
5	4
6	2

Copyright © Mometrix Media. You have been licensed one copy of this document for personal use only. Any other reproduction or redistribution is strictly prohibited. All rights reserved.

17. The data below was collected by repeating the same experiment four different times. What conclusion can be drawn based on the data shown?

Bicycle Obstacle Race

Student	Trial 1	Trial 2	Trial 3	Trial 4
Kayla	57.6 s	37.6 s	37.3 s	36.2 s
Carson	64.0 s	32.6 s	31.2 s	28.4 s
Jeremy	59.2 s	31.0 s	28.8 s	27.9 s
Rachel	61.3 s	42.6 s	39.5 s	39.0 s

Ⓐ The data was accurate in all four trials

Ⓑ The data in trials 2 through 4 is probably inaccurate

Ⓒ An error occurred in trial 1 that gave inaccurate data

Ⓓ The times in trial 4 are fastest because the students were tired

18. The first microscope was developed by Hans and Zacharias Janssen and allowed scientists to

Ⓐ See organisms too small to be seen with the naked eye

Ⓑ Count the number of organisms in the universe

Ⓒ Determine the causes of all human illness

Ⓓ Study why some females are taller than others

19. Electrical cords, such as the cords of a television or the cord on a toaster, are covered with rubber or plastic. What would you expect to happen if a portion of the rubber covering were missing when you tried to plug the cord in?

Ⓐ The appliance would not work after it was plugged in

Ⓑ The person plugging the appliance in would feel an electric shock

Ⓒ The appliance being plugged in would work, but all other appliances in the home would stop working

Ⓓ The cover does not matter, all appliances would work normally

20. Which of the statements below explains why a boy can run fast on the beach, but is much slower in water?

Ⓐ The boy is afraid of sharks and slows down when he enters the water

Ⓑ The boy cannot swim and stops running to avoid drowning

Ⓒ Water is thicker than air, which creates more resistance and slows the boy down

Ⓓ The force of the waves causes the boy to float, which prevents him from running

Copyright © Mometrix Media. You have been licensed one copy of this document for personal use only. Any other reproduction or redistribution is strictly prohibited. All rights reserved.

21. Place your answer on the provided griddable answer sheet.
In order to produce a constant supply of energy, solar panels require constant exposure to what?

22. Which statement accurately describes a state of matter?

    Ⓐ Solids take the shape of their container

    Ⓑ Gases maintain a fixed shape

    Ⓒ Liquids will expand to fill the volume of a container

    Ⓓ Gases expand to fill an entire space

23. Based on the weather forecast, what can a farmer expect to happen to his bird bath overnight?

10pm	11pm	12am	1am	2am	3am	4am	5am
34°C	25°C	11°C	2°C	-4 °C	-12 °C	-18°C	-18°C

    Ⓐ Freeze

    Ⓑ Evaporate

    Ⓒ Melt

    Ⓓ Sublime

24. The boiling point of water is 100°C. Adding salt raises the boiling point. What is the result of adding salt to water when cooking pasta?

    Ⓐ The pasta cooks more slowly

    Ⓑ The pasta will not stick together

    Ⓒ The water will boil more quickly

    Ⓓ The pasta will cook in hotter water

25. A man accidentally drops his wallet in a swimming pool. He can see his wallet at the bottom of the pool. He jumps in to retrieve it, but the wallet is not where it appeared to be. What is the reason for the optical illusion?

    Ⓐ The reflection of sunlight off of the water disrupted his view

    Ⓑ Light is refracted as it enters the water changing the wallet's apparent location

    Ⓒ The current at the bottom of the pool caused the wallet to move

    Ⓓ The heat from the Sun has impaired the man's vision

Copyright © Mometrix Media. You have been licensed one copy of this document for personal use only. Any other reproduction or redistribution is strictly prohibited. All rights reserved.

26. Two students spent several hours testing how well different running shoes supported athletes' feet. All of the following allow the students to effectively communicate the results of their experiment except

Ⓐ Create an advertisement that tells only the positive results of the shoes

Ⓑ Design a side by side comparison with graphs and conclusions that reveals all of the results of the experiment

Ⓒ Develop an oral report that presents their results

Ⓓ Write a paper that summarizes their experiment and results

27. The observations outlined below were made about a pot of water over a campfire. What is the most likely explanation for these observations?

- The pot was half full of water
- The pot hung over the campfire for 15 minutes
- The water began boiling after 7 minutes
- A white vapor was observed over the pot
- After 15 minutes, the pot was one quarter of the way full

Ⓐ Some of the water disappeared

Ⓑ The water changes from a gas to a liquid

Ⓒ Some of the water changed from a liquid to a gas, which was the vapor observed

Ⓓ The pot was never half full, someone measured incorrectly

28. A ball is resting on the front end of a boat. The boat is moving straight forwards toward a dock. When the front of the boat hits the dock, how will the ball's motion change?

Ⓐ The ball will remain at rest

Ⓑ The ball will move backwards

Ⓒ The ball will move forwards

Ⓓ The ball will move sideways

29. Which statement describes how fossil fuels are made?

Ⓐ Oil from Earth's core slowly rises to the Earth's surface and forms ponds

Ⓑ Lava within some volcanoes becomes so hot that is transforms into fossil fuels

Ⓒ Dead and decomposing organisms, exposed to extreme heat and pressure, transform into fossil fuels

Ⓓ When mountains form on top of coal, the pressure liquefies the coal creating fossil fuels

Copyright © Mometrix Media. You have been licensed one copy of this document for personal use only. Any other reproduction or redistribution is strictly prohibited. All rights reserved.

30. The Sahara desert receives about 3.6 inches of precipitation per year. Antarctica is also a desert receiving between 3 to 8 inches of precipitation per year. What makes an area a desert?

Ⓐ The temperature

Ⓑ The amount of animal life

Ⓒ The number of people living in the region

Ⓓ The yearly precipitation

31. What question are the students most likely testing with the experiment outlined below?

Seed type: Pansy Water: ½ gallon daily Soil: Bob's soil Daylight: 3 hours per day Flower color: Blue	Seed type: Pansy Water: ½ gallon daily Soil: Texas dirt Daylight: 3 hours per day Flower color: Purple	Seed type: Pansy Water: ½ gallon daily Soil: Grow Up Dirt Daylight: 3 hours per day Flower color: red

Ⓐ Does the amount of water affect how tall a flower will grow?

Ⓑ Does the type of soil affect the color of a flower?

Ⓒ What color of flower do bees prefer?

Ⓓ Is three hours of daylight enough for flowers to grow?

32. A prairie ecosystem is described below. Which organisms from the ecosystem are carnivores?

Grass is eaten by grasshoppers, rabbits, and crickets
Corn is eaten by squirrels and beetles
Grasshoppers, beetles, and crickets are all eaten by birds
Squirrels, birds, and rabbits are all eaten by both foxes and coyotes

Ⓐ Corn and grass

Ⓑ Grasshoppers and crickets

Ⓒ Beetles and birds

Ⓓ Foxes and coyotes

Copyright © Mometrix Media. You have been licensed one copy of this document for personal use only. Any other reproduction or redistribution is strictly prohibited. All rights reserved.

33. In a food chain, where does energy go after the secondary consumer dies?

Ⓐ Back to the Sun

Ⓑ To the producers

Ⓒ Into air, becomes wind

Ⓓ To decomposers

34. Every year thousands of square miles of trees are cut down to make paper products. Which of the following is not a result of cutting down trees?

Ⓐ Animals experience a loss of habitat

Ⓑ There is a decrease in the amount of oxygen available

Ⓒ There is a decrease in the amount of food available to herbivores and omnivores

Ⓓ There is a decrease in the amount of CO_2 in the atmosphere

35. According to the data below, what can be determined about Saturn?

Planet	Length of Year	Length of Day
Venus	224.7 days	116.75 days
Earth	365 days	24 hours
Saturn	10,759 days	10 hours 32 minutes
Neptune	164.79 years	16.11 hours

Ⓐ Saturn takes the least amount of time to rotate on its axis.

Ⓑ Saturn is the furthest planet from the Sun.

Ⓒ The further a planet is from the Sun, the shorter its day will be.

Ⓓ The larger a planet is, the longer its day will be.

36. A dog is an omnivore. What would you expect a dog's diet to consist of?

Ⓐ Meat

Ⓑ Vegetables

Ⓒ Both meat and vegetables

Ⓓ Neither meat nor vegetables

Copyright © Mometrix Media. You have been licensed one copy of this document for personal use only. Any other reproduction or redistribution is strictly prohibited. All rights reserved.

37. The following represents a simple food chain. What trophic level contains the greatest amount of energy?

Tree → Caterpillar → Frog → Snake → Hawk → Worm

(A) Tree

(B) Caterpillar

(C) Hawk

(D) Worm

38. How are organisms, such as snakes, cacti, and coyotes, able to survive in harsh desert conditions?

(A) Over thousands of years these organisms have developed adaptations to survive in arid climates

(B) These organisms migrate out of the desert during the summer months, only living in the desert for a portion of the year

(C) Snakes, cacti, and coyotes work together to find sources of food and water

(D) Snakes, cacti, and coyotes are all aquatic species that live in ponds and rivers during the hot day

39. A student is building a model of the Solar System using produce from the local supermarket. What order should she put the objects in to correctly represent the Solar System?

Object in Solar System	Model	Object in Solar System	Model
Mars	Raspberry	Uranus	tomato
Saturn	Grapefruit	Mercury	raisin
The Sun	Watermelon	Venus	grape
Jupiter	Lettuce	Asteroid Belt	sunflower seeds
Earth	Cherry	Neptune	orange

(A) Watermelon-raisin-grape-cherry-raspberry-tomato-orange-lettuce-grapefruit-seeds

(B) Watermelon-raisin-grape-cherry-raspberry-seeds-lettuce-grapefruit-tomato-orange

(C) Watermelon-lettuce-grapefruit-tomato-orange-cherry-grape-raspberry-raisin-seeds

(D) Watermelon-grape-raisin-cherry-seeds-raspberry-lettuce-grapefruti-orange-tomato

Copyright © Mometrix Media. You have been licensed one copy of this document for personal use only. Any other reproduction or redistribution is strictly prohibited. All rights reserved.

40. Why is it important to form a hypothesis before performing an experiment?

Ⓐ The experimenter will not have enough time to create a hypothesis after beginning the experiment

Ⓑ Developing a hypothesis ensures that the lab will be safe

Ⓒ The experiment will take too much time to complete if there is no hypothesis

Ⓓ The hypothesis tells what the experiment is going to be testing

41. A student is working on a science project and is going through each step of the scientific method. After the student conducts his or her first experiment and records the results of the experimental test, what should the student do next?

Ⓐ Communicate the results

Ⓑ Draw a conclusion

Ⓒ Repeat the experiment

Ⓓ Create a hypothesis

42. Which of the following is considered a non-renewable resource?

Ⓐ Glass

Ⓑ Wood

Ⓒ Cattle

Ⓓ Soil

43. How is force being applied to the box below?

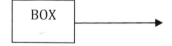

Ⓐ The box is being pulled forward

Ⓑ The box is being pushed forward

Ⓒ Gravity is forcing the box to move forward

Ⓓ Friction is forcing the box to stop

Copyright © Mometrix Media. You have been licensed one copy of this document for personal use only. Any other reproduction or redistribution is strictly prohibited. All rights reserved.

44. What is the benefit of a kangaroo's large ears?

Ⓐ They improve the kangaroo's vision

Ⓑ Large ears help kangaroos taste their food

Ⓒ Large ears allow kangaroos to outrun predators

Ⓓ Large ears help kangaroos hear predators coming

Copyright © Mometrix Media. You have been licensed one copy of this document for personal use only. Any other reproduction or redistribution is strictly prohibited. All rights reserved.

Answers and Explanations

1. B: Thermometers are used to measure temperature. Graduated cylinders are used to measure volume while a ruler is used to measure distance. Balances are used to measure mass.

2. C: Wheel A is turning clockwise, which causes wheel B to turn counterclockwise. Wheel B then causes wheel C to turn clockwise. Wheel C in turn, turns wheel D in the counterclockwise direction. The question states that the wheels are in contact, and the number of intermediate wheels does not prevent the turning motion from being transferred all the way down the line.

3. B: The east coast, states such as Maine, New York, and New Hampshire are three hours ahead of states on the west coast such as California, Washington, and Oregon. Earth rotates west to east, and that is counterclockwise when viewed from above the North Pole.

4. A: The human body works best within a certain temperature range, around 98.6°F. When the body gets too cold or too hot it cannot function properly. The boy who is outside in the winter is cold. His body temperature is dropping below 98.6°F. His muscles start to contract causing him to shiver in order to generate heat. The girl is outside in the summer, and begins sweating to reduce her body temperature from rising too far above 98.6°F. In both cases, the children's bodies are trying to keep the temperature close to 98.6°F.

5. A: Heat on Earth is generated by the Sun. The more direct sunlight an area on Earth receives from the Sun, the warmer it will be. When the Northern hemisphere is tilted away from the Sun, all of the countries in the Northern hemisphere experience winter. At that same time, the Southern hemisphere experiences summer. The same is true when the Southern hemisphere experiences winter; the Northern hemisphere experiences summer.

6. B: The advertisement states that Power Fruit contains 100% of the daily value of vitamin C, which means that it meets the amount of vitamin C a person needs each day. The ad also states that Power Fruit contains 35 mg of caffeine, but there is no indication of what the daily value of caffeine is. There is no mention of vitamin A or iron anywhere in the advertisement.

7. D: Glaciers and ice caps are fresh water unavailable for human use as they are frozen. The hydrologic cycle refers to all the water on planet Earth. Some water is in forms that humans do not tend to use, such as oceans (too salty and expensive to desalinate) and glaciers. Water suitable for drinking can be found as surface water and in ground water, which is obtained through wells. Answers A, Rivers, B, Estuaries, and C, Aquifers, are all examples of surface water that are available to humans.

8. D: Igneous rocks are formed when magma in Earth erupts through cracks in the crust where it cools creating a hard structure with many air pockets or holes.

9. A: Anytime there is an accident in the lab, the first step is always to tell the teacher. Even if a student or students were doing something that they should not have been doing, such as

Copyright © Mometrix Media. You have been licensed one copy of this document for personal use only. Any other reproduction or redistribution is strictly prohibited. All rights reserved.

horse playing in the lab, the teacher's first priority is still to make sure the students are safe. Telling the teacher will allow him or her to respond appropriately to the situation and make sure that all of the students remain safe.

10. B: The air we breathe is composed of many types of molecules, and is quite heavy compared to helium. The reason helium balloons float is because helium is less dense than the surrounding air. Objects that are less dense will float in objects that are more dense, as a helium balloon does when surrounded by air.

11. C: The prefix *carni-* means flesh, so carnivores are flesh eaters. Their diet consists of meats. The only answer choice that is a meat is an animal.

12. A: Plants are considered producers because they are able to absorb light energy from the Sun and convert it into food through the process of photosynthesis. In other words, plants are producers because they produce their own food from sunlight.

13. A: The volume of a graduated cylinder should be read at the bottom of the meniscus.

14. A: Turn it into an "if/then" statement. A formalized hypothesis written in the form of an if/then statement can then be tested. A statement may make a prediction or imply a cause/effect relationship, but that does not necessarily make it a good hypothesis. In this example, having the student rewrite the statement in the form of an if/then statement could read: If the length of the string of the pendulum is varied, then the time it takes the ball to make one complete period changes. This hypothesis is testable, doesn't simply make a prediction, nor does it give a conclusion. The validity of the hypothesis can then be supported or disproved by experimentation and observation.

15. C: Laboratory instructions not only contain steps to the procedure, but also often contain important safety information. The instructions should always be read before beginning the lab. Any questions should be addressed by the instructor before starting an experiment.

16. D: The graph represents a set of data. The line graph increases in distance from 1 second to 4 seconds and then begins decreasing. The only data set that shows distance increasing and then decreasing is set D.

17. C: The data is relatively consistent with the exception of trial 1. When an experiment is repeated using the same process multiple times, the data from each trial should be very similar or the same. The results of trial 1 indicate that an error may have occurred in the procedure yielding inaccurate results.

18. A: The microscope was discovered when a series of lenses were placed in a specific order magnifying objects that were too small to see otherwise. The development of the microscope also led to discoveries such as the cell, bacteria, and fungi.

19. B: The purpose of the rubber coating on the outside of electrical cords is to contain the electric current in the metal wire. When part of the rubber coating is missing, the electric current can leave the wire and cause an electric shock to the person plugging in the wire.

Copyright © Mometrix Media. You have been licensed one copy of this document for personal use only. Any other reproduction or redistribution is strictly prohibited. All rights reserved.

20. C: Water is denser than air and creates more resistance on the boy running. Air is thin and this allows the boy to run fast on the beach.

21. Sun: The word *solar* refers to the sun. Solar panels are large panels that absorb energy from the sun and convert it into other types of energy, such as electrical energy, that can be used to power anything from a car to a toaster. If there is no sun, such as at night, the panels do not take in any solar energy to convert to electricity. The amount of energy each solar panel can produce depends on the amount of sunlight it is exposed to.

22. D: The molecules that make up gases are far apart and move about very quickly. Because they have a weak attraction to each other, they expand to take up as much space as possible.

23. A: The weather forecast shows that a cold front will be arriving in the area causing the temperature to drop from 34°C to -18°C. The freezing point of water is 0°C, which means that the water in the birdbath will freeze overnight after the cold front arrives.

24. D: Adding salt to water causes the boiling point of water to rise. The water has to reach a temperature beyond 100°C in order to boil, so the water will be hotter when the pasta cooks. It is a common misconception that because the salt water is boiling at a higher temperature, the pasta will cook faster. The increase in temperature is too slight to make a significant difference in cooking time.

25. B: Light travels faster in air than it can in water. Water molecules are closer together than air particles are, which causes the light to slow down and bend as it enters the water. The bending of light is called refraction and creates the illusion of the wallet being next to where it actually is.

26. A: The purpose of a scientific experiment is to collect as much reliable data as possible about a specific hypothesis. Scientists can use the results from other experiments to help them determine what hypothesis to test next. Creating an advertisement that tells only the positive aspects of the running shoes would omit any negative aspects of the shoes that may be relevant. The results would not be reliable because they would be incomplete.

27. C: Water boils at 100°C. As the pot of water heats up over the campfire, it begins to boil causing the liquid water to turn into water vapor, a gas. The vapor the campers observed over the boiling pot of water was water vapor. As the water continues to boil, more of the liquid turns into gas resulting in a decrease in the volume of water in the pot.

28. C: The ball will move forwards. The ball is moving forward with the boat. When the front of the boat hits the dock, the ball's motion does not change. It continues to move forward because the force acting to stop the boat is not acting upon the ball. The forward motion of the boat is halted by the dock. The forward motion of the ball is not stopped. Since the ball is round there is little friction to provide an equal and opposite reaction to the forward motion.

29. C: Organisms that lived millions of years ago have been covered up by many layers of earth. The temperature and pressure increases transforming the dead organisms into fossil fuels that can be obtained and used for energy.

Copyright © Mometrix Media. You have been licensed one copy of this document for personal use only. Any other reproduction or redistribution is strictly prohibited. All rights reserved.

30. D: A desert is classified by the average amount of precipitation the region receives on a yearly basis. The temperature is irrelevant, as there are both hot and cold deserts. Due to the dry conditions, only organisms designed to withstand the arid conditions can survive in these areas.

31. B: In order to determine the question being tested, you must look at the data given. Answer choice A asks about how tall a flower will grow, but the height of the flowers is not given, so this cannot be what was tested. Answer choice C asks about bees, which are also not referenced anywhere in the experiment. Answer choice D asks about the amount of daylight required for the flowers to grow. All three flowers were given the same amount of daylight- three hours, so this cannot be what is tested. The only change between each of the tests is the type of dirt used, which affected the flower color.

32. D: Carnivores eat meat only. In the ecosystem described, both coyotes and foxes are carnivores eating squirrels, birds, and rabbits.

33. D: After a secondary consumer dies, such as a wolf, its body is partially consumed by decomposers, such as bacteria and fungi. Bacteria and fungi live in soil and digest body tissues of dead organisms converting them into basic nutrients that plants need to grow. Therefore, after secondary consumers die, their energy is consumed by decomposers, who make nutrients available in the soil for producers to use. *Do not confuse nutrients in the soil with energy that producers get from the Sun to make their own food.*

34. D: Trees absorb and use carbon dioxide to produce their own food. Humans breathe in oxygen and breathe out carbon dioxide. To a human, too much carbon dioxide is toxic and can cause serious problems. Plants use carbon dioxide and release oxygen as waste. This allows what is toxic to humans, carbon dioxide, to be used and transformed into breathable oxygen. A decrease in the number of trees decreases the amount of plants taking in carbon dioxide, causing the carbon dioxide levels in the atmosphere to rise.

35. A: When a planet rotates on its axis it creates day and night. The side of the planet that faces away from the Sun is in night. When that side rotates around to face the Sun, it is in day. The data indicates that Saturn takes the least amount of time to rotate on its axis, which indicates that is has the shortest day at only 10 hours and 32 minutes.

36. C: The prefix *omni*-means all, so an omnivore eats all types of food. Omnivores, such as dogs and many humans, eat a variety of plants and meats to achieve a balanced diet.

37. A: In the food chain of Tree → Caterpillar → Frog → Snake → Hawk → Worm, the tree is at the trophic level with the greatest amount of energy. Trophic level refers to the position of an organism in a food chain. Energy is lost according to the laws of thermodynamics as one moves up the food chain because it is converted to heat when consumers consume. Primary producers, such as autotrophs, are organisms who are at the base and capture solar energy. Primary consumers are herbivores that feed on the producers. Secondary consumers consume primary consumers and so on. Decomposers get their energy from the consumption of dead plants and animals.

38. A: Many organisms, especially organisms that live in harsh conditions such as deserts or frozen icy areas, have developed specific adaptations that allow them to survive. For

Copyright © Mometrix Media. You have been licensed one copy of this document for personal use only. Any other reproduction or redistribution is strictly prohibited. All rights reserved.

example, cacti are able to expand to store large amounts of water, coyotes absorb some water from their food, and snakes can escape the heat by hiding within rocks.

39. B: This question is really asking you to determine the correct order of the major bodies in the Solar System. The correct order is: Sun (watermelon), Mercury (raisin), Venus (grape), Earth (cherry), Mars (raspberry), asteroid belt (seeds), Jupiter (lettuce), Saturn (grapefruit), Uranus (tomato), Neptune (orange).

40. D: A hypothesis predicts what the experimenter thinks is going to happen and why. It is based on prior knowledge and research. An experiment is designed to test the hypothesis. Without a hypothesis, an experiment cannot be designed or performed.

41. C: Repeating the experiment validates data. Each separate experiment is called a repetition. Results of experiments or tests should be able to be replicated. Similar data gathered from many experiments can also be used to quantify the validity of the hypothesis. Repeating the experiments allows the student to observe variation in the results. Variation in data can be caused by a variety of errors or may be disproving the hypothesis. Answer D, Create a hypothesis, comes before experiments. Answers A, Communicate the results, and B, Draw a conclusion, occur after testing.

42. A: Glass is considered a non-renewable resource. Glass is manufactured and can be recycled, but is considered a non-renewable resource. Answer B, Wood, is considered a renewable resource because with proper management, an equilibrium can be reached between harvesting trees and planting new ones. Cattle, Answer C, are managed in herds and a balance can be achieved between those consumed and those born. Answer D, Soil, is the result of long-term erosion and includes organic matter and minerals needed by plants. Soil found naturally in the environment is renewed. Crops can be rotated to help maintain a healthy soil composition for farming.

43. A: The picture shows an arrow in front of the box pulling the box forward. If the box were being pushed, the arrow would be behind the box pushing it forward. Gravity pulls downward, not forward.

44. D: Kangaroos live in a dry, wide-open environment where there is little coverage from predators. It is important for kangaroos to be able to hear predators coming from a far distance so they can escape. Their large ears help them to hear subtle sounds of potential predators from far away.

Copyright © Mometrix Media. You have been licensed one copy of this document for personal use only. Any other reproduction or redistribution is strictly prohibited. All rights reserved.

Practice Test #2

Practice Questions

1. A prairie ecosystem is described below. Farmers treat fields surrounding the prairie with pesticides that kill part of the beetle population. What effect would the pesticides have on the rest of the ecosystem?

Grass is eaten by grasshoppers, rabbits, and crickets

Corn is eaten by squirrels and beetles

Grasshoppers, beetles, and crickets are all eaten by birds

Squirrels, birds, and rabbits are all eaten by both foxes and coyotes

Ⓐ There would be a decrease in the cricket population.

Ⓑ There would be an increase in the population of birds.

Ⓒ The population of rabbits would decrease.

Ⓓ The population of foxes would increase.

2. Which organisms from the ecosystem described above are herbivores?

Ⓐ Corn and grass

Ⓑ Grasshoppers and crickets

Ⓒ Beetles and birds

Ⓓ Foxes and coyotes

3. Which statement correctly describes the relationship between plants and animals?

Ⓐ Animals breathe in oxygen and plants release oxygen.

Ⓑ Animals breathe in carbon dioxide while plants release carbon dioxide.

Ⓒ Animals breathe in carbon dioxide while plants breathe out carbon dioxide.

Ⓓ Animals get oxygen from plants by eating the plants.

- 67 -

Copyright © Mometrix Media. You have been licensed one copy of this document for personal use only. Any other reproduction or redistribution is strictly prohibited. All rights reserved.

4. Which picture best represents Earth's position on its axis?

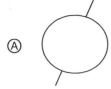
Ⓐ

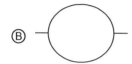
Ⓑ

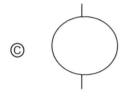
Ⓒ

Ⓓ

5. What should be included in a hypothesis?

    Ⓐ A hypothesis should tell what you think is going to happen and why.

    Ⓑ A hypothesis should state what the results of similar experiments were.

    Ⓒ A hypothesis should summarize the results of an experiment.

    Ⓓ A hypothesis should compare the control to the variable.

6. What causes high and low tide?

    Ⓐ The Earth's rotation

    Ⓑ The Moon's gravity

    Ⓒ The wind currents

    Ⓓ The change in water temperature

Copyright © Mometrix Media. You have been licensed one copy of this document for personal use only. Any other reproduction or redistribution is strictly prohibited. All rights reserved.

7. Earth rotates on its axis every 24 hours and revolves around the Sun every 365 earth days. Mars revolves around the Sun every 687 earth days. What does a period 687 earth days represent in terms of Mars time?

    (A) One Martian day

    (B) One Martian year

    (C) One Martian season

    (D) One Martian month

8. What does a food chain show?

    (A) The flow of energy between organisms

    (B) Very type of species living in a habitat

    (C) The population of each species in a habitat

    (D) The number of offspring a species will produce in a year

9. Lions live in savannah and grassland regions where there are tall dry grasses. Lions must sneak up and stalk their prey. What is the most likely reason for a lion's sand colored coat?

    (A) It allows lions to hide within the grass

    (B) The light color of their coat reflects heat from the Sun

    (C) A lion's coloring helps it attract mates

    (D) It allows them to run faster than their prey

10. In which of the following scenarios is Mario not applying work to a book?

    (A) Mario moves a book from the floor to the top shelf of a bookcase

    (B) Mario lets go of a book that he is holding so that it falls to the floor

    (C) Mario pushes a box of books across the room

    (D) Mario balances a book on his head and walks across the room

11. Wind farms are one source of alternative energy, energy that can be used in place of fossil fuels. The amount of energy a wind farm produces is determined by

    (A) Sunlight

    (B) Season

    (C) Wind

    (D) Rainfall

Copyright © Mometrix Media. You have been licensed one copy of this document for personal use only. Any other reproduction or redistribution is strictly prohibited. All rights reserved.

12. A carnivore would eat all of the following except

Ⓐ Rabbits

Ⓑ Acorns

Ⓒ Fish

Ⓓ Deer

13. What instrument should be used to measure how fast a boy can run 100 meters?

Ⓐ Beaker

Ⓑ Meterstick

Ⓒ Stopwatch

Ⓓ Thermometer

14. Students have just completed a lab. What can they do to be sure that their results are reliable?

Ⓐ Repeat the lab again

Ⓑ Compare their data to data collected in similar experiments

Ⓒ Measure all of their results twice with two different rulers

Ⓓ Make sure that their results confirm that their hypothesis was correct

15. What would be the best material to make a cooking pot out of?

Ⓐ Rubber

Ⓑ Copper

Ⓒ Plastic

Ⓑ Cement

16. Flowers, trees, and shrubs are all examples of what?

Ⓐ Carnivores

Ⓑ Herbivores

Ⓒ Producers

Ⓓ Predators

Copyright © Mometrix Media. You have been licensed one copy of this document for personal use only. Any other reproduction or redistribution is strictly prohibited. All rights reserved.

17. Why can a person see their reflection in a mirror?

Ⓐ Light is scattered when it hits a mirror producing a backward image

Ⓑ Light is reflected off of the mirror back towards the person standing in front of it

Ⓒ Light bends as it passes through the mirror creating an optical illusion

Ⓓ Light is refracted, which produces a mirror image behind the glass

18. A tropical flower is planted in a local garden. The garden is watered 2 to 3 times per week during all seasons. After only a few months the tropical plant begins to droop and turn brown. How did environmental change most likely affect the tropical plant?

Ⓐ Being watered 2 to 3 times per week was not enough to sustain a tropical plant

Ⓑ The new environment was too hot and burned the plant

Ⓒ Insects attacked the plant causing it to wilt

Ⓓ The new soil lacked the nutrients necessary to maintain the plant's health

19. Place your answer on the provided griddable answer sheet.
How many planets are in Earth's solar system?

20. What type of satellite is Pluto?

Ⓐ Planet

Ⓑ Comet

Ⓒ Dwarf planet

Ⓓ Asteroid

21. Algae are part of many food chains. How do algae produce energy?

algae   fish   seal   shark

Ⓐ They hunt fish for food

Ⓑ Algae undergo photosynthesis

Ⓒ They decompose dead or dying organisms

Ⓓ They consume fossil fuel from beneath Earth's surface

Copyright © Mometrix Media. You have been licensed one copy of this document for personal use only. Any other reproduction or redistribution is strictly prohibited. All rights reserved.

22. Four windows are washed with different cleaners. The same paper towel is used on each. The squares below show each window before being cleaned. What is the variable in the experiment?

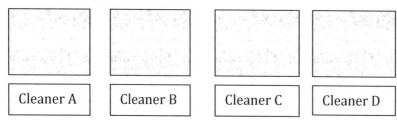

Cleaner A	Cleaner B	Cleaner C	Cleaner D

Ⓐ The amount of sunlight coming through the windows

Ⓑ The type of window cleaner used

Ⓒ The amount of dirt on each window

Ⓓ The type of paper towel used

23. Why is it more difficult to push a shopping cart full of groceries than an empty shopping cart?

Ⓐ The full cart has less mass than the empty cart

Ⓑ The full cart has a greater mass than the empty cart

Ⓒ The full cart has less friction than the empty cart

Ⓓ The empty cart is not pulled down by gravity

24. Use the information in the table to determine what would happen to the mass and weight of a human if he or she were on Neptune.

Mass	Mass is the amount of matter there is. Mass only changes when matter is added or removed.
Weight	Weight is how much gravity pulls downward on an object. The more gravity there is, the more an object weighs.
Gravity on Earth: 9.8 m/s²	Gravity on Neptune: 11.15 m/s²

Ⓐ A person's mass and weight would increase on Neptune

Ⓑ A person's mass and weight would decrease on Neptune

Ⓒ A person's mass would increase, but weight would be unchanged

Ⓓ A person's mass would be unchanged, but weight would increase

Copyright © Mometrix Media. You have been licensed one copy of this document for personal use only. Any other reproduction or redistribution is strictly prohibited. All rights reserved.

25. Look at the two images of a spring shown below. The first is a spring before it has been stretched by a force. The second is the same spring after it has been stretched by a force. Use your ruler to determine how far the force caused the spring to stretch?

Before Force

After force

Ⓐ 0.2 cm

Ⓑ 0.5 cm

Ⓒ 1.0 cm

Ⓓ 1.5 cm

26. How are the size of a dog and the pitch of its bark related?

Breed	Height from ground to back	Pitch of Bark
Chihuahua	20 cm	17 Hz
Cocker Spaniel	45 cm	14 Hz
Labrador	63 cm	12 Hz
Dalmatian	78 cm	11 Hz
Great Dane	114 cm	8 Hz

Ⓐ The smaller breeds have a lower pitch bark than the larger breeds

Ⓑ The size of the dog has no relationship to the pitch of the bark

Ⓒ The larger breeds have a lower pitch bark than the smaller breeds

Ⓓ The smallest breed and largest breed have the highest pitch barks

27. How are we able to see the Moon on a dark night?

Ⓐ The Moon reflects light from the Sun, which illuminates the Moon

Ⓑ The Moon generates energy that makes it glow

Ⓒ The Moon reflects heat from the Sun that causes it to glow

Ⓓ The Moon's surface is covered in active volcanoes that glow when they erupt

Copyright © Mometrix Media. You have been licensed one copy of this document for personal use only. Any other reproduction or redistribution is strictly prohibited. All rights reserved.

28. In the diagram shown below, four wheels are in contact such that each wheel turns the opposite direction from the wheels it is touching. Wheel A is being turned clockwise by a force as shown. What direction is wheel C turning?

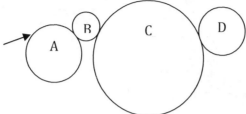

Ⓐ Wheel C does not turn at all because it is too much larger than wheel B

Ⓑ Wheel C does not turn at all because it is not touching wheel B

Ⓒ Wheel C turns counterclockwise

Ⓓ Wheel C turns clockwise

29. Water is stored underground, as well as in oceans and ice caps. Such underground storage reservoirs are called:

Ⓐ Storage tanks

Ⓑ Aquifers

Ⓒ Evaporators

Ⓓ Runoff

30. An ice cube tray is filled with water. The tray is placed in a freezer for 12 hours. The water freezes forming ice. The tray is removed from the freezer and left on a counter for 12 hours. What changes as the water becomes ice and then melts back into water?

Ⓐ The amount of energy in the water

Ⓑ The amount of water in the ice cube tray

Ⓒ The number of water molecules

Ⓓ The mass of the water molecules

Copyright © Mometrix Media. You have been licensed one copy of this document for personal use only. Any other reproduction or redistribution is strictly prohibited. All rights reserved.

31. Several people were asked to jump on a large trampoline, one at a time, to see who could jump the highest. The results were recorded in the data table below.

Person	Weight	Highest Jump
Sarah	59 kg	1.35 m
Mark	75 kg	1.81 m
Isaac	78 kg	1.93 m
Valerie	64 kg	1.47 m
Crystal	66 kg	1.57 m

Based on the data, what can be concluded about the relationship between weight and jumping height?

Ⓐ The more a person weighs, the higher he or she could jump

Ⓑ The less a person weighs, the higher he or she could jump

Ⓒ A person's weight does not affect how high he or she was able to jump

Ⓓ The taller the person is, the higher he or she could jump

32. Which statement describes how Earth's relationship to the Sun allows the polar ice caps to remain frozen?

Ⓐ The equator receives the most direct sunlight while the poles receive the least amount of sunlight

Ⓑ The Moon reflects the Sun's light away from the North and South Pole preventing them from heating up

Ⓒ Wind currents constantly move air warmed by the Sun away from the North and South Pole and toward the equator

Ⓓ The Sun does not shine on the North or South Pole so they never warm up

33. A Tsunami may be caused by:

Ⓐ Earthquakes

Ⓑ Volcanoes

Ⓒ Landslides

Ⓓ A, B, and C

34. Which piece of safety equipment is designed to protect your eyes?

Ⓐ Glasses

Ⓑ Goggles

Ⓒ Gloves

Ⓓ Eye wash

Copyright © Mometrix Media. You have been licensed one copy of this document for personal use only. Any other reproduction or redistribution is strictly prohibited. All rights reserved.

35. How is force being applied to the box below?

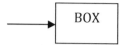 BOX

Ⓐ The box is being pulled forward

Ⓑ The box is being pushed forward

Ⓒ Gravity is forcing the box to move forward

Ⓓ Friction is forcing the box to stop

36. Your teacher gives you a beaker of water and a beaker of vinegar. Both liquids are clear. What is the best way to distinguish between the two liquids?

Ⓐ Take a small sip of each liquid, the vinegar will taste bad

Ⓑ Put your nose directly over each beaker and inhale deeply, the vinegar will smell bad

Ⓒ Add some baking soda to each beaker, the vinegar will react and form bubbles

Ⓓ Ask your teacher to label the beakers before handing them to you

37. Which of the following does not represent a physical change?

Ⓐ Salt dissolved in water

Ⓑ A spoiling apple

Ⓒ Sand dissolved in water

Ⓓ Pulverized rock

38. Polar bears, seals and walrus' are all arctic animals that have a thick layer of blubber or fat beneath their skin. What purpose does this layer of blubber serve?

Ⓐ Protects them from predators

Ⓑ Helps to preserve body heat

Ⓒ Aids in finding food

Ⓓ Prevents them from drowning in water

Copyright © Mometrix Media. You have been licensed one copy of this document for personal use only. Any other reproduction or redistribution is strictly prohibited. All rights reserved.

39. What does not need to be done after performing an experiment?

Ⓐ Wash hands

Ⓑ Brush hair

Ⓒ Clean up area

Ⓓ Complete the lab assignment

40. Why do some cacti have folds in their outer skin?

Ⓐ The folds can expand, allowing the cacti to absorb and store water when it rains

Ⓑ The folds help protect the cacti from predators

Ⓒ The folds allow them to absorb nutrients from the air

Ⓓ The folds provide support, allowing the cacti to grow tall

41. The factor most responsible for determining which season an area is experiencing is

Ⓐ Elevation

Ⓑ The position of the earth in its orbit around the sun

Ⓒ Latitude

Ⓓ Air masses

42. After a science laboratory exercise, some solutions remain unused and are left over. What should be done with these solutions?

Ⓐ Dispose of the solutions according to local disposal procedures

Ⓑ Empty the solutions into the sink and rinse with warm water and soap

Ⓒ Ensure the solutions are secured in closed containers and throw away

Ⓓ Store the solutions in a secured, dry place for later use

43. Compared to fresh water, the freezing point of sea water is

Ⓐ Higher

Ⓑ Lower

Ⓒ About the same

Ⓓ Sea water does not freeze

Copyright © Mometrix Media. You have been licensed one copy of this document for personal use only. Any other reproduction or redistribution is strictly prohibited. All rights reserved.

44. The formation of sedimentary rock includes all of the following processes except

Ⓐ Layering

Ⓑ Cementation

Ⓒ Compaction

Ⓓ Heat

Copyright © Mometrix Media. You have been licensed one copy of this document for personal use only. Any other reproduction or redistribution is strictly prohibited. All rights reserved.

Answers and Explanations

1. A: In the ecosystem described, birds eat beetles, crickets, and grasshoppers. If a pesticide were to kill off part of the beetle population, birds would be forced to consume more crickets and grasshoppers to meet their energy needs. As a result, there would be a decrease in the cricket population.

2. B: Herbivores are organisms that eat producers (plants) only. In the ecosystem described, both grasshoppers and crickets are herbivores, eating corn and grass.

3. A: Animals breathe in oxygen and breathe out carbon dioxide in a process called respiration. Plants use the carbon dioxide that animals exhale, in the process of photosynthesis, and convert it into oxygen.

4. A: Earth sits on its axis at a tilt of 23.4°. Choice B would result in Earth rotating sideways and choice C is straight up and down. Choice D is not even physically possible.

5. A: A hypothesis is an educated guess formulated by the experimenter based on prior experiments and research. A hypothesis includes what the experimenters think is going to happen and their reasoning.

6. B: Tides are caused by the effect of the Moon's gravity and the Sun's gravity pulling on the ocean waters.

7. B: A year is determined by the number of days it takes for a body to make one revolution around the Sun. So a Martian year would be the number of days it takes for Mars to orbit the Sun.

8. A: A food chain shows how energy flows from one consumer to another. The arrows point in the direction that energy moves. For example, if an arrow points from a flower to a bee, then the energy from the flower flows to the bee as the bee eats the nectar of the flower.

9. A: Lions live in a wide open area where there are few large objects to hide behind. In order to get close enough to their prey to chase and attack it, they must be able to sneak up on it. Their coloration is similar to the color of the tall grasses where they live. This allows the lions to blend into their surroundings and get close to their prey.

10. B: When Mario lets go of the book, he is no longer exerting any force on it, so he cannot be doing work on it. In all the other examples, Mario is exerting a force on the book in the direction that it is moving. In Answer A, Mario moves a book from the floor to the top shelf. Mario lifted up vertically on the book, in the same direction that the book moved, so he was doing work. In Answer C, Mario pushes a box of books across the room. This is also an example of work being done because the box moved in the direction of the force Mario applied. In Answer D, Mario is indirectly applying a horizontal force to the book because of the friction between the book and his head, so he is exerting a force on the book in the direction he is moving.

11. C: Wind farms harvest energy from wind to use in combination with or in place of fossil fuels. The biggest limiting factors for wind farms are the inconsistency and unpredictability

Copyright © Mometrix Media. You have been licensed one copy of this document for personal use only. Any other reproduction or redistribution is strictly prohibited. All rights reserved.

of wind and the difficulties involved in storing the energy that has been harvested. Wind farms can only produce as much energy as they receive from wind.

12. B: Carnivores eat meat only. The only choice that is not meat is acorns, which are plant products.

13. C: In this case, the term "how long" refers to the time it takes to do something, such as how long it takes a boy to run 100 meters. The instrument to measure time is a stopwatch.

14. A: To be the more precise, the students could complete the lab again. In fact, all scientific laws have been developed by being tested over and over again through repetitive scientific experiment.

15. B: A cooking pot must be able to conduct heat from the stove into the food being prepared. The only material that is a conductor from the choices given is copper.

16. C: Flowers, trees, and shrubs are all plants, which are producers. Producers are able to make their own food using energy from the Sun in a process known as photosynthesis.

17. B: A mirror is a reflective surface. The flat shiny surface reflects any incoming light allowing a person standing in front of the mirror to see their reflection.

18. A: Tropical environments typically receive rain 5 to 6 times per week, even if it is only a brief afternoon shower. In its new environment the tropical plant is not receiving enough water to survive.

19. There are eight planets in our solar system: Mercury, Venus, Earth, Mars, Jupiter, Saturn, Uranus, and Neptune.

20. C: Pluto was originally classified as a planet but in 2006, it was changed to a dwarf planet because of other similar type objects orbiting very close to it.

21. B: Algae are a type of plant that grows in water. Because algae are plants they are able to capture light from the Sun and transform it into energy during the process of photosynthesis.

22. B: A variable is something that is changed in the experiment. It is being tested against other similar things. In this experiment, the variable is the type of window cleaner.

23. B: The empty shopping cart does not weigh very much and is easy to push. As groceries are added to the empty cart, the cart gains mass. By the time the shopping cart is full, it has more mass than it began with and requires more force to push it.

24. D: The table states that a person's mass remains the same, but weight will fluctuate with the force of gravity. It also states that the more gravity acting on an object, the more the object will weigh. Neptune has a greater gravitational force than Earth, so the person's weight would increase.

25. B: The spring has a length of 1 cm before the force, and a length of 1.5 cm afterwards. The difference in lengths is 0.5 cm.

Copyright © Mometrix Media. You have been licensed one copy of this document for personal use only. Any other reproduction or redistribution is strictly prohibited. All rights reserved.

26. C: The table shows that the largest dogs have the lowest pitch barks ranging from 8 to 12 hertz. The smaller dogs, such as the Chihuahua and spaniel, have higher pitch barks of 17 and 14 hertz.

27. A: The Moon does not emit any light of its own. However, the Moon does reflect light from the Sun. The phase of the Moon that we are able to see on Earth, such as full moon, crescent, or no moon, depends on where the Moon is positioned in relation to the Sun and Earth.

28. D: Wheel A is turning clockwise, which causes wheel B to turn counterclockwise. Wheel B then causes wheel C to turn clockwise. The question states that the wheels are in contact, and while wheel C's size will cause it to rotate more slowly; it will not prevent it from turning.

29. B: An aquifer (a word derived from the Latin root *aqua*, meaning water) is any geologic formation containing ground water.

30. A: When water changes from a liquid to a solid the amount of thermal energy is decreasing. The molecules move closer together, which creates the solid crystal structure of the ice. As the ice melts back into a liquid, thermal energy level increases, causing the molecules to spread out again.

31. A: The table shows a clear correlation between mass and jump height. If you put the list of jumpers in order from highest mass to lowest mass, they will also be in order from highest jump height to lowest jump height. Choice D can be eliminated immediately because there is no information about any of the individuals' heights in the data table or in the question.

32. A: The equator receives the most direct sunlight while the North and South Pole receive the least amount of direct sunlight. In addition, the atmosphere helps to reflect some of the Sun's heat energy away from the poles. Finally, the reflectivity of the ice helps to deflect some of the heat away from the polar ice caps.

33. D: A tsunami, sometimes referred to as a tidal wave, is a large wave or series of waves caused by the displacement of a large volume of water. While the most common cause is an earthquake, large landslides (either falling into the sea or taking place under water) or explosive volcanic action may also result in a tsunami. Tsunamis take the appearance of very high, sustained tides, and may move water very far inland. Large storms, such as cyclones or hurricanes, may also displace great quantities of water, causing a high tide known as a storm surge that also resembles a tsunami.

34. B: Goggles are proper protective eyewear for laboratory. Glasses provide almost no protection as they could break and they are open around the sides where chemicals could splash into the eyes. An eye wash is used to rinse out eyes if chemicals accidently get splashed into them.

35. B: The picture shows an arrow behind the box pushing it forward. If the box were being pulled, the arrow would be in front of the box pulling the box forward. Gravity pulls downward, not forward.

Copyright © Mometrix Media. You have been licensed one copy of this document for personal use only. Any other reproduction or redistribution is strictly prohibited. All rights reserved.

36. D: Labeling beakers before adding fluids to them helps to ensure that the fluids are placed in correct containers and can be identified after being poured. Smelling, tasting, and adding chemicals other than those directed by your instructor are a violation of lab safety.

37. B: A spoiling apple has undergone a chemical change (one substance is changed into another). Dissolving both sand and salt in water, refers to a physical change, since the salt and water and the sand and water can be separated again by evaporating the water, which is a physical change. Pulverized rock is also an example of a physical change where the form has changed but not the substance itself.

38. B: Polar bears, seals, and walrus' all live in arctic climates where it is very cold all year round. The thick layer of blubber that these animals have below the surface of their skin helps them preserve body heat keeping them warm in the frigid environment.

39. B: Brushing hair is not a requirement after completing a laboratory assignment. Choice A, washing hands is required after every lab experiment in order to ensure that no chemicals or lab agents are ingested. Cleaning up the lab area ensures that all equipment is ready for the next experiment. Finishing the assignment is also necessary in order to draw a conclusion from the data collected.

40. A: Cacti live in a desert environment where water is scarce. When it rains, cacti must be able to absorb and store as much water as possible so that they have water available during the dry periods. The folds on the outside of a cactus allow it to expand and fill with water. After a heavy rain, cacti will appear round and plump because the folds are full of water.

41. B: As the earth travels around the sun, it tilts towards the sun or away from it, depending on where it is in its orbit. This tilt is what determines the seasons. The earth is tilted towards the sun in summer and away from it in winter. Elevation a. and latitude c. of an area remain constant throughout the year, so they cannot account for the changing of the seasons. Air masses d. can influence the weather, but don't determine the seasons.

42. A: Dispose of the solutions according to local disposal procedures. Solutions and compounds used in labs may be hazardous according to state and local regulatory agencies and should be treated with such precaution. Answer B, Empty the solutions into the sink and rinse with warm water and soap, does not take into account the hazards associated with a specific solution in terms of vapors, or interactions with water, soap and waste piping systems. Answer C, Ensure the solutions are secured in closed containers and throw away, may allow toxic chemicals to get into landfills and subsequently into fresh water systems. Answer D, Store the solutions in a secured, dry place for later use, is incorrect as chemicals should not be re-used due to the possibility of contamination.

43. B: The freezing point of sea water is lower than fresh water as sea water is more dense. It is more dense because it has more dissolved salts. The freezing point changes with salinity, pressure and density, but can be -2°C (28.4°F) compared with fresh water, 0°C (32°F). As sea water freezes, it forms pockets of high-salinity brine that do not freeze. The brine slowly leaches out of the sea water ice as it forms. When the ice eventually melts, it has a lesser degree of salinity.

Copyright © Mometrix Media. You have been licensed one copy of this document for personal use only. Any other reproduction or redistribution is strictly prohibited. All rights reserved.

44. D: The formation of sedimentary rock does not include heat. Of the three types of rock igneous, sedimentary and metamorphic, heat is essential to two: igneous and metamorphic. Sedimentary rocks are formed by sediments that get deposited and then compacted or cemented together. Sedimentary rocks are classified into detrital, organic or chemical sediments. Answer A, layering, is correct since sediments can be deposited or otherwise formed in layers. Answer B, cementation, is also called lithification. Answer C, compaction, refers to the pressure forming sedimentary rock leading to cementation.

Copyright © Mometrix Media. You have been licensed one copy of this document for personal use only. Any other reproduction or redistribution is strictly prohibited. All rights reserved.

Secret Key #1 - Time is Your Greatest Enemy

Pace Yourself

Wear a watch. At the beginning of the test, check the time (or start a chronometer on your watch to count the minutes), and check the time after every few questions to make sure you are "on schedule."

If you are forced to speed up, do it efficiently. Usually one or more answer choices can be eliminated without too much difficulty. Above all, don't panic. Don't speed up and just begin guessing at random choices. By pacing yourself, and continually monitoring your progress against your watch, you will always know exactly how far ahead or behind you are with your available time. If you find that you are one minute behind on the test, don't skip one question without spending any time on it, just to catch back up. Take 15 fewer seconds on the next four questions, and after four questions you'll have caught back up. Once you catch back up, you can continue working each problem at your normal pace.

Furthermore, don't dwell on the problems that you were rushed on. If a problem was taking up too much time and you made a hurried guess, it must be difficult. The difficult questions are the ones you are most likely to miss anyway, so it isn't a big loss. It is better to end with more time than you need than to run out of time.

Lastly, sometimes it is beneficial to slow down if you are constantly getting ahead of time. You are always more likely to catch a careless mistake by working more slowly than quickly, and among very high-scoring test takers (those who are likely to have lots of time left over), careless errors affect the score more than mastery of material.

Copyright © Mometrix Media. You have been licensed one copy of this document for personal use only. Any other reproduction or redistribution is strictly prohibited. All rights reserved.

Secret Key #2 - Guessing is not Guesswork

You probably know that guessing is a good idea. Unlike other standardized tests, there is no penalty for getting a wrong answer. Even if you have no idea about a question, you still have a 20-25% chance of getting it right.

Most test takers do not understand the impact that proper guessing can have on their score. Unless you score extremely high, guessing will significantly contribute to your final score.

Monkeys Take the Test

What most test takers don't realize is that to insure that 20-25% chance, you have to guess randomly. If you put 20 monkeys in a room to take this test, assuming they answered once per question and behaved themselves, on average they would get 20-25% of the questions correct. Put 20 test takers in the room, and the average will be much lower among guessed questions. Why?

1. The test writers intentionally write deceptive answer choices that "look" right. A test taker has no idea about a question, so he picks the "best looking" answer, which is often wrong. The monkey has no idea what looks good and what doesn't, so it will consistently be right about 20-25% of the time.
2. Test takers will eliminate answer choices from the guessing pool based on a hunch or intuition. Simple but correct answers often get excluded, leaving a 0% chance of being correct. The monkey has no clue, and often gets lucky with the best choice.

This is why the process of elimination endorsed by most test courses is flawed and detrimental to your performance. Test takers don't guess; they make an ignorant stab in the dark that is usually worse than random.

Copyright © Mometrix Media. You have been licensed one copy of this document for personal use only. Any other reproduction or redistribution is strictly prohibited. All rights reserved.

$5 Challenge

Let me introduce one of the most valuable ideas of this course—the $5 challenge:

You only mark your "best guess" if you are willing to bet $5 on it.
You only eliminate choices from guessing if you are willing to bet $5 on it.

Why $5? Five dollars is an amount of money that is small yet not insignificant, and can really add up fast (20 questions could cost you $100). Likewise, each answer choice on one question of the test will have a small impact on your overall score, but it can really add up to a lot of points in the end.

The process of elimination IS valuable. The following shows your chance of guessing it right:

If you eliminate wrong answer choices until only this many remain:	Chance of getting it correct:
1	100%
2	50%
3	33%

However, if you accidentally eliminate the right answer or go on a hunch for an incorrect answer, your chances drop dramatically—to 0%. By guessing among all the answer choices, you are GUARANTEED to have a shot at the right answer.

That's why the $5 test is so valuable. If you give up the advantage and safety of a pure guess, it had better be worth the risk.

What we still haven't covered is how to be sure that whatever guess you make is truly random. Here's the easiest way:

Always pick the first answer choice among those remaining.

Such a technique means that you have decided, **before you see a single test question**, exactly how you are going to guess, and since the order of choices tells you nothing about which one is correct, this guessing technique is perfectly random.

This section is not meant to scare you away from making educated guesses or eliminating choices; you just need to define when a choice is worth eliminating. The $5 test, along with a pre-defined random guessing strategy, is the best way to make sure you reap all of the benefits of guessing.

Copyright © Mometrix Media. You have been licensed one copy of this document for personal use only. Any other reproduction or redistribution is strictly prohibited. All rights reserved.

Secret Key #3 - Practice Smarter, Not Harder

Many test takers delay the test preparation process because they dread the awful amounts of practice time they think necessary to succeed on the test. We have refined an effective method that will take you only a fraction of the time.

There are a number of "obstacles" in the path to success. Among these are answering questions, finishing in time, and mastering test-taking strategies. All must be executed on the day of the test at peak performance, or your score will suffer. The test is a mental marathon that has a large impact on your future.

Just like a marathon runner, it is important to work your way up to the full challenge. So first you just worry about questions, and then time, and finally strategy:

Success Strategy

1. Find a good source for practice tests.
2. If you are willing to make a larger time investment, consider using more than one study guide. Often the different approaches of multiple authors will help you "get" difficult concepts.
3. Take a practice test with no time constraints, with all study helps, "open book." Take your time with questions and focus on applying strategies.
4. Take a practice test with time constraints, with all guides, "open book."
5. Take a final practice test without open material and with time limits.

If you have time to take more practice tests, just repeat step 5. By gradually exposing yourself to the full rigors of the test environment, you will condition your mind to the stress of test day and maximize your success.

Copyright © Mometrix Media. You have been licensed one copy of this document for personal use only. Any other reproduction or redistribution is strictly prohibited. All rights reserved.

Secret Key #4 - Prepare, Don't Procrastinate

Let me state an obvious fact: if you take the test three times, you will probably get three different scores. This is due to the way you feel on test day, the level of preparedness you have, and the version of the test you see. Despite the test writers' claims to the contrary, some versions of the test WILL be easier for you than others.

Since your future depends so much on your score, you should maximize your chances of success. In order to maximize the likelihood of success, you've got to prepare in advance. This means taking practice tests and spending time learning the information and test taking strategies you will need to succeed.

Never go take the actual test as a "practice" test, expecting that you can just take it again if you need to. Take all the practice tests you can on your own, but when you go to take the official test, be prepared, be focused, and do your best the first time!

Copyright © Mometrix Media. You have been licensed one copy of this document for personal use only. Any other reproduction or redistribution is strictly prohibited. All rights reserved.

Secret Key #5 - Test Yourself

Everyone knows that time is money. There is no need to spend too much of your time or too little of your time preparing for the test. You should only spend as much of your precious time preparing as is necessary for you to get the score you need.

Once you have taken a practice test under real conditions of time constraints, then you will know if you are ready for the test or not.

If you have scored extremely high the first time that you take the practice test, then there is not much point in spending countless hours studying. You are already there.

Benchmark your abilities by retaking practice tests and seeing how much you have improved. Once you consistently score high enough to guarantee success, then you are ready.

If you have scored well below where you need, then knuckle down and begin studying in earnest. Check your improvement regularly through the use of practice tests under real conditions. Above all, don't worry, panic, or give up. The key is perseverance!

Then, when you go to take the test, remain confident and remember how well you did on the practice tests. If you can score high enough on a practice test, then you can do the same on the real thing.

Copyright © Mometrix Media. You have been licensed one copy of this document for personal use only. Any other reproduction or redistribution is strictly prohibited. All rights reserved.

General Strategies

The most important thing you can do is to ignore your fears and jump into the test immediately. Do not be overwhelmed by any strange-sounding terms. You have to jump into the test like jumping into a pool—all at once is the easiest way.

Make Predictions

As you read and understand the question, try to guess what the answer will be. Remember that several of the answer choices are wrong, and once you begin reading them, your mind will immediately become cluttered with answer choices designed to throw you off. Your mind is typically the most focused immediately after you have read the question and digested its contents. If you can, try to predict what the correct answer will be. You may be surprised at what you can predict.

Quickly scan the choices and see if your prediction is in the listed answer choices. If it is, then you can be quite confident that you have the right answer. It still won't hurt to check the other answer choices, but most of the time, you've got it!

Answer the Question

It may seem obvious to only pick answer choices that answer the question, but the test writers can create some excellent answer choices that are wrong. Don't pick an answer just because it sounds right, or you believe it to be true. It MUST answer the question. Once you've made your selection, always go back and check it against the question and make sure that you didn't misread the question and that the answer choice does answer the question posed.

Benchmark

After you read the first answer choice, decide if you think it sounds correct or not. If it doesn't, move on to the next answer choice. If it does, mentally mark that answer choice. This doesn't mean that you've definitely selected it as your answer choice, it just means that it's the best you've seen thus far. Go ahead and read the next choice. If the next choice is worse than the one you've already selected, keep going to the next answer choice. If the next choice is better than the choice you've already selected, mentally mark the new answer choice as your best guess.

The first answer choice that you select becomes your standard. Every other answer choice must be benchmarked against that standard. That choice is correct until proven otherwise by another answer choice beating it out. Once you've decided that no other answer choice seems as good, do one final check to ensure that your answer choice answers the question posed.

Valid Information

Don't discount any of the information provided in the question. Every piece of information may be necessary to determine the correct answer. None of the information in the question is there to throw you off (while the answer choices will certainly have information to throw you off). If two seemingly unrelated topics are discussed, don't ignore either. You can be confident there is a relationship, or it wouldn't be included in the question, and you are probably going to have to determine what is that relationship to find the answer.

Copyright © Mometrix Media. You have been licensed one copy of this document for personal use only. Any other reproduction or redistribution is strictly prohibited. All rights reserved.

Avoid "Fact Traps"

Don't get distracted by a choice that is factually true. Your search is for the answer that answers the question. Stay focused and don't fall for an answer that is true but irrelevant. Always go back to the question and make sure you're choosing an answer that actually answers the question and is not just a true statement. An answer can be factually correct, but it MUST answer the question asked. Additionally, two answers can both be seemingly correct, so be sure to read all of the answer choices, and make sure that you get the one that BEST answers the question.

Milk the Question

Some of the questions may throw you completely off. They might deal with a subject you have not been exposed to, or one that you haven't reviewed in years. While your lack of knowledge about the subject will be a hindrance, the question itself can give you many clues that will help you find the correct answer. Read the question carefully and look for clues. Watch particularly for adjectives and nouns describing difficult terms or words that you don't recognize. Regardless of whether you completely understand a word or not, replacing it with a synonym, either provided or one you more familiar with, may help you to understand what the questions are asking. Rather than wracking your mind about specific detailed information concerning a difficult term or word, try to use mental substitutes that are easier to understand.

The Trap of Familiarity

Don't just choose a word because you recognize it. On difficult questions, you may not recognize a number of words in the answer choices. The test writers don't put "make-believe" words on the test, so don't think that just because you only recognize all the words in one answer choice that that answer choice must be correct. If you only recognize words in one answer choice, then focus on that one. Is it correct? Try your best to determine if it is correct. If it is, that's great. If not, eliminate it. Each word and answer choice you eliminate increases your chances of getting the question correct, even if you then have to guess among the unfamiliar choices.

Eliminate Answers

Eliminate choices as soon as you realize they are wrong. But be careful! Make sure you consider all of the possible answer choices. Just because one appears right, doesn't mean that the next one won't be even better! The test writers will usually put more than one good answer choice for every question, so read all of them. Don't worry if you are stuck between two that seem right. By getting down to just two remaining possible choices, your odds are now 50/50. Rather than wasting too much time, play the odds. You are guessing, but guessing wisely because you've been able to knock out some of the answer choices that you know are wrong. If you are eliminating choices and realize that the last answer choice you are left with is also obviously wrong, don't panic. Start over and consider each choice again. There may easily be something that you missed the first time and will realize on the second pass.

Tough Questions

If you are stumped on a problem or it appears too hard or too difficult, don't waste time. Move on! Remember though, if you can quickly check for obviously incorrect answer choices, your chances of guessing correctly are greatly improved. Before you completely

Copyright © Mometrix Media. You have been licensed one copy of this document for personal use only. Any other reproduction or redistribution is strictly prohibited. All rights reserved.

give up, at least try to knock out a couple of possible answers. Eliminate what you can and then guess at the remaining answer choices before moving on.

Brainstorm

If you get stuck on a difficult question, spend a few seconds quickly brainstorming. Run through the complete list of possible answer choices. Look at each choice and ask yourself, "Could this answer the question satisfactorily?" Go through each answer choice and consider it independently of the others. By systematically going through all possibilities, you may find something that you would otherwise overlook. Remember though that when you get stuck, it's important to try to keep moving.

Read Carefully

Understand the problem. Read the question and answer choices carefully. Don't miss the question because you misread the terms. You have plenty of time to read each question thoroughly and make sure you understand what is being asked. Yet a happy medium must be attained, so don't waste too much time. You must read carefully, but efficiently.

Face Value

When in doubt, use common sense. Always accept the situation in the problem at face value. Don't read too much into it. These problems will not require you to make huge leaps of logic. The test writers aren't trying to throw you off with a cheap trick. If you have to go beyond creativity and make a leap of logic in order to have an answer choice answer the question, then you should look at the other answer choices. Don't overcomplicate the problem by creating theoretical relationships or explanations that will warp time or space. These are normal problems rooted in reality. It's just that the applicable relationship or explanation may not be readily apparent and you have to figure things out. Use your common sense to interpret anything that isn't clear.

Prefixes

If you're having trouble with a word in the question or answer choices, try dissecting it. Take advantage of every clue that the word might include. Prefixes and suffixes can be a huge help. Usually they allow you to determine a basic meaning. Pre- means before, post- means after, pro - is positive, de- is negative. From these prefixes and suffixes, you can get an idea of the general meaning of the word and try to put it into context. Beware though of any traps. Just because con- is the opposite of pro-, doesn't necessarily mean congress is the opposite of progress!

Hedge Phrases

Watch out for critical hedge phrases, led off with words such as "likely," "may," "can," "sometimes," "often," "almost," "mostly," "usually," "generally," "rarely," and "sometimes." Question writers insert these hedge phrases to cover every possibility. Often an answer choice will be wrong simply because it leaves no room for exception. Unless the situation calls for them, avoid answer choices that have definitive words like "exactly," and "always."

Switchback Words

Stay alert for "switchbacks." These are the words and phrases frequently used to alert you to shifts in thought. The most common switchback word is "but." Others include "although," "however," "nevertheless," "on the other hand," "even though," "while," "in spite of," "despite," and "regardless of."

Copyright © Mometrix Media. You have been licensed one copy of this document for personal use only. Any other reproduction or redistribution is strictly prohibited. All rights reserved.

New Information

Correct answer choices will rarely have completely new information included. Answer choices typically are straightforward reflections of the material asked about and will directly relate to the question. If a new piece of information is included in an answer choice that doesn't even seem to relate to the topic being asked about, then that answer choice is likely incorrect. All of the information needed to answer the question is usually provided for you in the question. You should not have to make guesses that are unsupported or choose answer choices that require unknown information that cannot be reasoned from what is given.

Time Management

On technical questions, don't get lost on the technical terms. Don't spend too much time on any one question. If you don't know what a term means, then odds are you aren't going to get much further since you don't have a dictionary. You should be able to immediately recognize whether or not you know a term. If you don't, work with the other clues that you have—the other answer choices and terms provided—but don't waste too much time trying to figure out a difficult term that you don't know.

Contextual Clues

Look for contextual clues. An answer can be right but not the correct answer. The contextual clues will help you find the answer that is most right and is correct. Understand the context in which a phrase or statement is made. This will help you make important distinctions.

Don't Panic

Panicking will not answer any questions for you; therefore, it isn't helpful. When you first see the question, if your mind goes blank, take a deep breath. Force yourself to mechanically go through the steps of solving the problem using the strategies you've learned.

Pace Yourself

Don't get clock fever. It's easy to be overwhelmed when you're looking at a page full of questions, your mind is full of random thoughts and feeling confused, and the clock is ticking down faster than you would like. Calm down and maintain the pace that you have set for yourself. As long as you are on track by monitoring your pace, you are guaranteed to have enough time for yourself. When you get to the last few minutes of the test, it may seem like you won't have enough time left, but if you only have as many questions as you should have left at that point, then you're right on track!

Answer Selection

The best way to pick an answer choice is to eliminate all of those that are wrong, until only one is left and confirm that is the correct answer. Sometimes though, an answer choice may immediately look right. Be careful! Take a second to make sure that the other choices are not equally obvious. Don't make a hasty mistake. There are only two times that you should stop before checking other answers. First is when you are positive that the answer choice you have selected is correct. Second is when time is almost out and you have to make a quick guess!

Copyright © Mometrix Media. You have been licensed one copy of this document for personal use only. Any other reproduction or redistribution is strictly prohibited. All rights reserved.

Check Your Work

Since you will probably not know every term listed and the answer to every question, it is important that you get credit for the ones that you do know. Don't miss any questions through careless mistakes. If at all possible, try to take a second to look back over your answer selection and make sure you've selected the correct answer choice and haven't made a costly careless mistake (such as marking an answer choice that you didn't mean to mark). The time it takes for this quick double check should more than pay for itself in caught mistakes.

Beware of Directly Quoted Answers

Sometimes an answer choice will repeat word for word a portion of the question or reference section. However, beware of such exact duplication. It may be a trap! More than likely, the correct choice will paraphrase or summarize a point, rather than being exactly the same wording.

Slang

Scientific sounding answers are better than slang ones. An answer choice that begins "To compare the outcomes..." is much more likely to be correct than one that begins "Because some people insisted..."

Extreme Statements

Avoid wild answers that throw out highly controversial ideas that are proclaimed as established fact. An answer choice that states the "process should used in certain situations, if..." is much more likely to be correct than one that states the "process should be discontinued completely." The first is a calm rational statement and doesn't even make a definitive, uncompromising stance, using a hedge word "if" to provide wiggle room, whereas the second choice is a radical idea and far more extreme.

Answer Choice Families

When you have two or more answer choices that are direct opposites or parallels, one of them is usually the correct answer. For instance, if one answer choice states "x increases" and another answer choice states "x decreases" or "y increases," then those two or three answer choices are very similar in construction and fall into the same family of answer choices. A family of answer choices consists of two or three answer choices, very similar in construction, but often with directly opposite meanings. Usually the correct answer choice will be in that family of answer choices. The "odd man out" or answer choice that doesn't seem to fit the parallel construction of the other answer choices is more likely to be incorrect.

Copyright © Mometrix Media. You have been licensed one copy of this document for personal use only. Any other reproduction or redistribution is strictly prohibited. All rights reserved.

Special Report: How to Overcome Test Anxiety

The very nature of tests caters to some level of anxiety, nervousness, or tension, just as we feel for any important event that occurs in our lives. A little bit of anxiety or nervousness can be a good thing. It helps us with motivation, and makes achievement just that much sweeter. However, too much anxiety can be a problem, especially if it hinders our ability to function and perform.

"Test anxiety," is the term that refers to the emotional reactions that some test-takers experience when faced with a test or exam. Having a fear of testing and exams is based upon a rational fear, since the test-taker's performance can shape the course of an academic career. Nevertheless, experiencing excessive fear of examinations will only interfere with the test-taker's ability to perform and chance to be successful.

There are a large variety of causes that can contribute to the development and sensation of test anxiety. These include, but are not limited to, lack of preparation and worrying about issues surrounding the test.

Lack of Preparation

Lack of preparation can be identified by the following behaviors or situations:

Not scheduling enough time to study, and therefore cramming the night before the test or exam
Managing time poorly, to create the sensation that there is not enough time to do everything
Failing to organize the text information in advance, so that the study material consists of the entire text and not simply the pertinent information
Poor overall studying habits

Worrying, on the other hand, can be related to both the test taker, or many other factors around him/her that will be affected by the results of the test. These include worrying about:

Previous performances on similar exams, or exams in general
How friends and other students are achieving
The negative consequences that will result from a poor grade or failure

There are three primary elements to test anxiety. Physical components, which involve the same typical bodily reactions as those to acute anxiety (to be discussed below). Emotional factors have to do with fear or panic. Mental or cognitive issues concerning attention spans and memory abilities.

Copyright © Mometrix Media. You have been licensed one copy of this document for personal use only. Any other reproduction or redistribution is strictly prohibited. All rights reserved.

Physical Signals

There are many different symptoms of test anxiety, and these are not limited to mental and emotional strain. Frequently there are a range of physical signals that will let a test taker know that he/she is suffering from test anxiety. These bodily changes can include the following:

Perspiring
Sweaty palms
Wet, trembling hands
Nausea
Dry mouth
A knot in the stomach
Headache
Faintness
Muscle tension
Aching shoulders, back and neck
Rapid heart beat
Feeling too hot/cold

To recognize the sensation of test anxiety, a test-taker should monitor him/herself for the following sensations:

The physical distress symptoms as listed above
Emotional sensitivity, expressing emotional feelings such as the need to cry or laugh too much, or a sensation of anger or helplessness
A decreased ability to think, causing the test-taker to blank out or have racing thoughts that are hard to organize or control.

Though most students will feel some level of anxiety when faced with a test or exam, the majority can cope with that anxiety and maintain it at a manageable level. However, those who cannot are faced with a very real and very serious condition, which can and should be controlled for the immeasurable benefit of this sufferer.

Naturally, these sensations lead to negative results for the testing experience. The most common effects of test anxiety have to do with nervousness and mental blocking.

Nervousness

Nervousness can appear in several different levels:

The test-taker's difficulty, or even inability to read and understand the questions on the test
The difficulty or inability to organize thoughts to a coherent form
The difficulty or inability to recall key words and concepts relating to the testing questions (especially essays)
The receipt of poor grades on a test, though the test material was well known by the test taker

Copyright © Mometrix Media. You have been licensed one copy of this document for personal use only. Any other reproduction or redistribution is strictly prohibited. All rights reserved.

Conversely, a person may also experience mental blocking, which involves:

Blanking out on test questions
Only remembering the correct answers to the questions when the test has already finished.

Fortunately for test anxiety sufferers, beating these feelings, to a large degree, has to do with proper preparation. When a test taker has a feeling of preparedness, then anxiety will be dramatically lessened.

The first step to resolving anxiety issues is to distinguish which of the two types of anxiety are being suffered. If the anxiety is a direct result of a lack of preparation, this should be considered a normal reaction, and the anxiety level (as opposed to the test results) shouldn't be anything to worry about. However, if, when adequately prepared, the test-taker still panics, blanks out, or seems to overreact, this is not a fully rational reaction. While this can be considered normal too, there are many ways to combat and overcome these effects.

Remember that anxiety cannot be entirely eliminated, however, there are ways to minimize it, to make the anxiety easier to manage. Preparation is one of the best ways to minimize test anxiety. Therefore the following techniques are wise in order to best fight off any anxiety that may want to build.

To begin with, try to avoid cramming before a test, whenever it is possible. By trying to memorize an entire term's worth of information in one day, you'll be shocking your system, and not giving yourself a very good chance to absorb the information. This is an easy path to anxiety, so for those who suffer from test anxiety, cramming should not even be considered an option.

Instead of cramming, work throughout the semester to combine all of the material which is presented throughout the semester, and work on it gradually as the course goes by, making sure to master the main concepts first, leaving minor details for a week or so before the test.

To study for the upcoming exam, be sure to pose questions that may be on the examination, to gauge the ability to answer them by integrating the ideas from your texts, notes and lectures, as well as any supplementary readings.

If it is truly impossible to cover all of the information that was covered in that particular term, concentrate on the most important portions, that can be covered very well. Learn these concepts as best as possible, so that when the test comes, a goal can be made to use these concepts as presentations of your knowledge.

In addition to study habits, changes in attitude are critical to beating a struggle with test anxiety. In fact, an improvement of the perspective over the entire test-taking experience can actually help a test taker to enjoy studying and therefore improve the overall experience. Be certain not to overemphasize the significance of the grade - know that the result of the test is neither a reflection of self worth, nor is it a measure of intelligence; one grade will not predict a person's future success.

Copyright © Mometrix Media. You have been licensed one copy of this document for personal use only. Any other reproduction or redistribution is strictly prohibited. All rights reserved.

To improve an overall testing outlook, the following steps should be tried:

Keeping in mind that the most reasonable expectation for taking a test is to expect to try to demonstrate as much of what you know as you possibly can.
Reminding ourselves that a test is only one test; this is not the only one, and there will be others.
The thought of thinking of oneself in an irrational, all-or-nothing term should be avoided at all costs.
A reward should be designated for after the test, so there's something to look forward to. Whether it be going to a movie, going out to eat, or simply visiting friends, schedule it in advance, and do it no matter what result is expected on the exam.

Test-takers should also keep in mind that the basics are some of the most important things, even beyond anti-anxiety techniques and studying. Never neglect the basic social, emotional and biological needs, in order to try to absorb information. In order to best achieve, these three factors must be held as just as important as the studying itself.

Study Steps

Remember the following important steps for studying:

Maintain healthy nutrition and exercise habits. Continue both your recreational activities and social pass times. These both contribute to your physical and emotional well being.
Be certain to get a good amount of sleep, especially the night before the test, because when you're overtired you are not able to perform to the best of your best ability.
Keep the studying pace to a moderate level by taking breaks when they are needed, and varying the work whenever possible, to keep the mind fresh instead of getting bored. When enough studying has been done that all the material that can be learned has been learned, and the test taker is prepared for the test, stop studying and do something relaxing such as listening to music, watching a movie, or taking a warm bubble bath.

There are also many other techniques to minimize the uneasiness or apprehension that is experienced along with test anxiety before, during, or even after the examination. In fact, there are a great deal of things that can be done to stop anxiety from interfering with lifestyle and performance. Again, remember that anxiety will not be eliminated entirely, and it shouldn't be. Otherwise that "up" feeling for exams would not exist, and most of us depend on that sensation to perform better than usual. However, this anxiety has to be at a level that is manageable.

Of course, as we have just discussed, being prepared for the exam is half the battle right away. Attending all classes, finding out what knowledge will be expected on the exam, and knowing the exam schedules are easy steps to lowering anxiety. Keeping up with work will remove the need to cram, and efficient study habits will eliminate wasted time. Studying should be done in an ideal location for concentration, so that it is simple to become interested in the material and give it complete attention. A method such as SQ3R (Survey, Question, Read, Recite, Review) is a wonderful key to follow to make sure that the study habits are as effective as possible, especially in the case of learning from a

Copyright © Mometrix Media. You have been licensed one copy of this document for personal use only. Any other reproduction or redistribution is strictly prohibited. All rights reserved.

textbook. Flashcards are great techniques for memorization. Learning to take good notes will mean that notes will be full of useful information, so that less sifting will need to be done to seek out what is pertinent for studying. Reviewing notes after class and then again on occasion will keep the information fresh in the mind. From notes that have been taken summary sheets and outlines can be made for simpler reviewing.

A study group can also be a very motivational and helpful place to study, as there will be a sharing of ideas, all of the minds can work together, to make sure that everyone understands, and the studying will be made more interesting because it will be a social occasion.

Basically, though, as long as the test-taker remains organized and self confident, with efficient study habits, less time will need to be spent studying, and higher grades will be achieved.

To become self confident, there are many useful steps. The first of these is "self talk." It has been shown through extensive research, that self-talk for students who suffer from test anxiety, should be well monitored, in order to make sure that it contributes to self confidence as opposed to sinking the student. Frequently the self talk of test-anxious students is negative or self-defeating, thinking that everyone else is smarter and faster, that they always mess up, and that if they don't do well, they'll fail the entire course. It is important to decreasing anxiety that awareness is made of self talk. Try writing any negative self thoughts and then disputing them with a positive statement instead. Begin self-encouragement as though it was a friend speaking. Repeat positive statements to help reprogram the mind to believing in successes instead of failures.

Helpful Techniques

Other extremely helpful techniques include:

Self-visualization of doing well and reaching goals
While aiming for an "A" level of understanding, don't try to "overprotect" by setting your expectations lower. This will only convince the mind to stop studying in order to meet the lower expectations.
Don't make comparisons with the results or habits of other students. These are individual factors, and different things work for different people, causing different results.
Strive to become an expert in learning what works well, and what can be done in order to improve. Consider collecting this data in a journal.
Create rewards for after studying instead of doing things before studying that will only turn into avoidance behaviors.
Make a practice of relaxing - by using methods such as progressive relaxation, self-hypnosis, guided imagery, etc - in order to make relaxation an automatic sensation.
Work on creating a state of relaxed concentration so that concentrating will take on the focus of the mind, so that none will be wasted on worrying.
Take good care of the physical self by eating well and getting enough sleep.
Plan in time for exercise and stick to this plan.

Copyright © Mometrix Media. You have been licensed one copy of this document for personal use only. Any other reproduction or redistribution is strictly prohibited. All rights reserved.

Beyond these techniques, there are other methods to be used before, during and after the test that will help the test-taker perform well in addition to overcoming anxiety.

Before the exam comes the academic preparation. This involves establishing a study schedule and beginning at least one week before the actual date of the test. By doing this, the anxiety of not having enough time to study for the test will be automatically eliminated. Moreover, this will make the studying a much more effective experience, ensuring that the learning will be an easier process. This relieves much undue pressure on the test-taker.

Summary sheets, note cards, and flash cards with the main concepts and examples of these main concepts should be prepared in advance of the actual studying time. A topic should never be eliminated from this process. By omitting a topic because it isn't expected to be on the test is only setting up the test-taker for anxiety should it actually appear on the exam. Utilize the course syllabus for laying out the topics that should be studied. Carefully go over the notes that were made in class, paying special attention to any of the issues that the professor took special care to emphasize while lecturing in class. In the textbooks, use the chapter review, or if possible, the chapter tests, to begin your review.

It may even be possible to ask the instructor what information will be covered on the exam, or what the format of the exam will be (for example, multiple choice, essay, free form, true-false). Additionally, see if it is possible to find out how many questions will be on the test. If a review sheet or sample test has been offered by the professor, make good use of it, above anything else, for the preparation for the test. Another great resource for getting to know the examination is reviewing tests from previous semesters. Use these tests to review, and aim to achieve a 100% score on each of the possible topics. With a few exceptions, the goal that you set for yourself is the highest one that you will reach.

Take all of the questions that were assigned as homework, and rework them to any other possible course material. The more problems reworked, the more skill and confidence will form as a result. When forming the solution to a problem, write out each of the steps. Don't simply do head work. By doing as many steps on paper as possible, much clarification and therefore confidence will be formed. Do this with as many homework problems as possible, before checking the answers. By checking the answer after each problem, a reinforcement will exist, that will not be on the exam. Study situations should be as exam-like as possible, to prime the test-taker's system for the experience. By waiting to check the answers at the end, a psychological advantage will be formed, to decrease the stress factor.

Another fantastic reason for not cramming is the avoidance of confusion in concepts, especially when it comes to mathematics. 8-10 hours of study will become one hundred percent more effective if it is spread out over a week or at least several days, instead of doing it all in one sitting. Recognize that the human brain requires time in order to assimilate new material, so frequent breaks and a span of study time over several days will be much more beneficial.

Additionally, don't study right up until the point of the exam. Studying should stop a minimum of one hour before the exam begins. This allows the brain to rest and put

Copyright © Mometrix Media. You have been licensed one copy of this document for personal use only. Any other reproduction or redistribution is strictly prohibited. All rights reserved.

things in their proper order. This will also provide the time to become as relaxed as possible when going into the examination room. The test-taker will also have time to eat well and eat sensibly. Know that the brain needs food as much as the rest of the body. With enough food and enough sleep, as well as a relaxed attitude, the body and the mind are primed for success.

Avoid any anxious classmates who are talking about the exam. These students only spread anxiety, and are not worth sharing the anxious sentimentalities.

Before the test also involves creating a positive attitude, so mental preparation should also be a point of concentration. There are many keys to creating a positive attitude. Should fears become rushing in, make a visualization of taking the exam, doing well, and seeing an A written on the paper. Write out a list of affirmations that will bring a feeling of confidence, such as "I am doing well in my English class," "I studied well and know my material," "I enjoy this class." Even if the affirmations aren't believed at first, it sends a positive message to the subconscious which will result in an alteration of the overall belief system, which is the system that creates reality.

If a sensation of panic begins, work with the fear and imagine the very worst! Work through the entire scenario of not passing the test, failing the entire course, and dropping out of school, followed by not getting a job, and pushing a shopping cart through the dark alley where you'll live. This will place things into perspective! Then, practice deep breathing and create a visualization of the opposite situation - achieving an "A" on the exam, passing the entire course, receiving the degree at a graduation ceremony.

On the day of the test, there are many things to be done to ensure the best results, as well as the most calm outlook. The following stages are suggested in order to maximize test-taking potential:

Begin the examination day with a moderate breakfast, and avoid any coffee or beverages with caffeine if the test taker is prone to jitters. Even people who are used to managing caffeine can feel jittery or light-headed when it is taken on a test day.
Attempt to do something that is relaxing before the examination begins. As last minute cramming clouds the mastering of overall concepts, it is better to use this time to create a calming outlook.
Be certain to arrive at the test location well in advance, in order to provide time to select a location that is away from doors, windows and other distractions, as well as giving enough time to relax before the test begins.
Keep away from anxiety generating classmates who will upset the sensation of stability and relaxation that is being attempted before the exam.
Should the waiting period before the exam begins cause anxiety, create a self-distraction by reading a light magazine or something else that is relaxing and simple.

During the exam itself, read the entire exam from beginning to end, and find out how much time should be allotted to each individual problem. Once writing the exam, should more time be taken for a problem, it should be abandoned, in order to begin another problem. If there is time at the end, the unfinished problem can always be returned to and completed.

Copyright © Mometrix Media. You have been licensed one copy of this document for personal use only. Any other reproduction or redistribution is strictly prohibited. All rights reserved.

Read the instructions very carefully - twice - so that unpleasant surprises won't follow during or after the exam has ended.

When writing the exam, pretend that the situation is actually simply the completion of homework within a library, or at home. This will assist in forming a relaxed atmosphere, and will allow the brain extra focus for the complex thinking function.

Begin the exam with all of the questions with which the most confidence is felt. This will build the confidence level regarding the entire exam and will begin a quality momentum. This will also create encouragement for trying the problems where uncertainty resides.

Going with the "gut instinct" is always the way to go when solving a problem. Second guessing should be avoided at all costs. Have confidence in the ability to do well.

For essay questions, create an outline in advance that will keep the mind organized and make certain that all of the points are remembered. For multiple choice, read every answer, even if the correct one has been spotted - a better one may exist.

Continue at a pace that is reasonable and not rushed, in order to be able to work carefully. Provide enough time to go over the answers at the end, to check for small errors that can be corrected.

Should a feeling of panic begin, breathe deeply, and think of the feeling of the body releasing sand through its pores. Visualize a calm, peaceful place, and include all of the sights, sounds and sensations of this image. Continue the deep breathing, and take a few minutes to continue this with closed eyes. When all is well again, return to the test.

If a "blanking" occurs for a certain question, skip it and move on to the next question. There will be time to return to the other question later. Get everything done that can be done, first, to guarantee all the grades that can be compiled, and to build all of the confidence possible. Then return to the weaker questions to build the marks from there.

Remember, one's own reality can be created, so as long as the belief is there, success will follow. And remember: anxiety can happen later, right now, there's an exam to be written!

After the examination is complete, whether there is a feeling for a good grade or a bad grade, don't dwell on the exam, and be certain to follow through on the reward that was promised...and enjoy it! Don't dwell on any mistakes that have been made, as there is nothing that can be done at this point anyway.

Additionally, don't begin to study for the next test right away. Do something relaxing for a while, and let the mind relax and prepare itself to begin absorbing information again.

From the results of the exam - both the grade and the entire experience, be certain to learn from what has gone on. Perfect studying habits and work some more on confidence in order to make the next examination experience even better than the last one.

Copyright © Mometrix Media. You have been licensed one copy of this document for personal use only. Any other reproduction or redistribution is strictly prohibited. All rights reserved.

Learn to avoid places where openings occurred for laziness, procrastination and day dreaming.

Use the time between this exam and the next one to better learn to relax, even learning to relax on cue, so that any anxiety can be controlled during the next exam. Learn how to relax the body. Slouch in your chair if that helps. Tighten and then relax all of the different muscle groups, one group at a time, beginning with the feet and then working all the way up to the neck and face. This will ultimately relax the muscles more than they were to begin with. Learn how to breathe deeply and comfortably, and focus on this breathing going in and out as a relaxing thought. With every exhale, repeat the word "relax."

As common as test anxiety is, it is very possible to overcome it. Make yourself one of the test-takers who overcome this frustrating hindrance.

Copyright © Mometrix Media. You have been licensed one copy of this document for personal use only. Any other reproduction or redistribution is strictly prohibited. All rights reserved.

Additional Bonus Material

Due to our efforts to try to keep this book to a manageable length, we've created a link that will give you access to all of your additional bonus material.

Please visit http://www.mometrix.com/bonus948/fsag5sci to access the information.

Copyright © Mometrix Media. You have been licensed one copy of this document for personal use only. Any other reproduction or redistribution is strictly prohibited. All rights reserved.

BOCA RATON PUBLIC LIBRARY, FLORIDA

3 3656 0648890 9

J 372.35076 Mom
Mometrix Exam Secrets Test
 Prep Team.
Florida state assessments
 grade 5 science [...]

DEC   2016